MANIFESTING MODERN MIRACLES

MANIFESTING MODERN MIRACLES

MANIFESTING MODERN MIRACLES

ISBN: 978-0-9961389-2-5

Ordering information: Quantity Sales. Special discounts are available on quantity purchases by corporations, associations, and others. For details, contact the Special Sales Department at Visionary Insight Press.

Visionary Insight Press
822 Westchester Place
Charleston, IL 61920

Visionary Insight Press, the Visionary Insight Press logo and its individual parts are trademarks of Visionary Insight Press.

Compiled by: Lisa Hardwick

Back cover photo credit: Rick Pickford, Jase White, ASM Studios, Teresa Bolinski at T. Bolinski Photography, Ryan Jay of Ryan Jay Photography, Alisa Dawn Photography, Susan Chantal Photography, Anthony Mendonca, Cindy Moleski Photography, Michael Gonzalez/El Creative, Duygu Ozen of Moments Photography Studio, Patrick Jones Studios, Sydney. Photographer Chris Walsh, Christy Westrom, Kaydin Carlsen, ABC Studios, Annie Bee's Photography.

Table of Contents

Foreword

by Elizabeth A.A.Wilson

Manifesting Modern Miracles is a book brimming with enlightenment and encouragement. The stories within are awe-inspiring and rewarding. What makes this book such a valuable resource is the simple fact that these are real stories authored by real people chronicling real miracles in everyday life. A simple and powerful reminder that divinity is everywhere.

Everyone has, whether they realize it or not, a story to tell of miracles. I've believed in miracles my whole life. Of course, because I believed in them I also saw them; I experienced miracles fully time and time again as I grew up. From sudden flashes of inspiration to full-blown out of this world miraculous manifestations, I've seen them everywhere and always. Every time I experienced a miracle it would strengthen my faith in them, which of course would attract greater and greater miracles. And so on.

I've realized where my unshakable belief in miracles has come from. It's from the greatest lesson my mom ever taught me: *It'll always be alright in the end.* Those simple and comforting words might seem to some a bit naïve, but to me they laid the foundation for a lifetime of knowing that no problem was ever too big to be solved. No situation too sticky, no bully too strong. No dream unachievable. In fact, I don't think even she knew the magnitude of what she had taught me. The words weren't just comforting, they were the key to living without fear.

She was my mother, so I believed her. And for that reason, every problem I ever encountered always miraculously worked itself out. Somehow, it really *was* always alright in the end. There were my miracles, thousands of them.

Conditioning is such a huge part of how we think, and therefore what we experience. We most often speak of conditioning as a bad thing, referencing the limiting and fear-inducing wisdom we inherit from parents, teachers, politicians and so on. We know that children who grow up being told they'll never amount to much rarely do, and that children who grow up in volatile homes are more likely to experience violence as adults. But the same is true the other way around. The miracles I've experienced in my life were both a gift from the divine but also my own doing—because I had been conditioned both by my mother and by the evidential experiences I had as a result of her wisdom to believe so fully in miracles that the Universe had no choice but to manifest them for me.

So I lived with the conditioned belief that miracles come about when needed, but it took me a good number of years to understand how. It took a while to understand that life is a craft that can be mastered, and the same Infinite Power that produces miracles is the Power that flows through us and steers our lives in the direction of our thinking.

What ignited my journey to this understanding was a simple question from my husband. We had recently moved from England to the United States with a 6-week old daughter, leaving behind a stable decade-long career in business strategy. I was in a new home, in a new country, with a new baby, and the future was wide open ahead of me. I had no path to tread, no tracks to follow, and the sheer width of the horizon was overwhelming.

"So what do you want to do?" he asked.

With no pre-approved answer available in my archives of *The-Way-It-Is*, I had no choice but to put some thought to it. Like a kick to the gut I suddenly remembered what I'd *always* wanted to do. And it wasn't business strategy. I wanted to write a book.

"*But it's so hard to get published,*" said Fear-Of-Failure.

"*You can't come up with a story that hasn't been told before,*" said Inadequacy.

"*And authors don't make any money, it's probably best to stick to business,*" said Common Sense.

"Do it!!" said my husband.

Up until that point nothing professional had inspired me at all, which is of course why my working life had been stagnant for so long. But now my mother's words danced to the tune of my soul song, finally playing loud enough for me to hear it. Somehow it would work out. It had to, because it always does. Some miracle would make it work.

So, with no experience or any idea of how I was going to achieve anything, I picked up a pen. Since then I've enjoyed many successes, including collaborating with *New York Times* bestselling authors, scoring a book deal with Simon & Schuster, publishing two novels, landing a job doing the narrative development for a new Nintendo 8-Bit fantasy game, starring in a documentary and travelling to distant lands for the filming. I even got to meet and interview my hero, 41 times bestselling fantasy author Piers Anthony.

"*You were in the right place at the right time, that's all,*" said Sceptic. And it's true. Even Piers Anthony himself told me that to succeed as an author you need to be extraordinarily lucky. But I was so fascinated by how my success had come about that I embarked on a mission to understand exactly what 'luck' is. After hundreds of books in hundreds of fields, from science to theology, this is my conclusion:

'Luck' is the craft of being available for miracles to occur.

That was the key to it all. My mother's wisdom had created a pattern of thinking that truly set me up to be a successful co-creator of my life. When I reached this realization I went from being solidly agnostic to becoming deeply spiritual and a minister of metaphysics.

So how do we master this craft?

The answer is written within this book, hidden in the pages of these inspiring stories. And, as was the case with **Amy Pazahanick** as written in her chapter "*A Birthday Miracle*", sometimes all it takes is a book to get us on our way.

There is a very specific process involved in allowing miracles to take form in our lives, lyrically but truthfully laid out in "*Tending Mind's Garden*" by **Lisa Spooner**. Of course, although the process is universal, our approach to that process must necessarily be unique to us. The chapter by **Tonia Browne**, "*Minting Miracles*", is a useful tool for remembering the steps, and **Vandana Mendonca** provides in her chapter, "*Soul Miracles*", some examples of the personalized nature of our approach to the process.

The first step is to believe that miracles are even possible. As we learn in the chapter by **Angela N. Holton**, "*Believe, Expect, Receive*", miracles are simply the signs of God's work, the essence of Divine movement to and through us. The power we wield as human extensions of this Divine movement is beyond expression, though a thought-provoking summary is provided in **Catherine Madeira's** chapter "*Structures of Life*". Small or big, miracles are as real and as common as other unseen elements like air or ether. These are metaphysical principles that align with modern science, but whether you achieve this faith through prayer, meditation, or scientific study doesn't matter. The scientist who thinks about life as an unfolding of possibilities in an eternal quantum field of potential knows that reality is nothing more than one's perspective. The theologian who knows that all things, from thought to matter, come from the same unformed substance known as the Body of God is sure to realize he is as capable of miracles as his Creator. The psychologist who understands that subconscious paradigms drive our actions far more than our desires do knows that a reconditioning of our thinking can drastically alter our experience. Even adults can condition their habitual thought patterns to produce results so miraculous their faith will strengthen daily, not unlike the miracle of transformation told beautifully in **Tracy Carlson's** "*Everyday Miracles*". A paradigm shift, caused by the slightest adjustment in our perception, is enough to cause a ripple effect that soon has us totally immersed in the business of creation. A colorful example of total immersion is found in **Barbara McKay's** *"My Ford F150 XTR Super Crew"*.

The second step is to release resistance. Most people would probably deny being 'resistant' to miraculous results, but in truth it can be very hard to operate our lives in alignment with divine flow, especially if we don't know what that flow feels like. Frustration, bitterness, boredom, stress, anger and so on are all a breeding ground for negative thoughts, and by learning to let go of these and remaining undisturbed by inharmonious situations we release destructive power and let only one force the space to operate within us: the Divine power. The chapter by **Antoinette Coleman-Kelly**, *"Stepping Delightfully Forward"*, is a demonstration of the incredible results achievable by 'letting go'. One of the greatest lessons in this regard is found in the chapter by **Kelly Vass**, *"She Chose Happily Ever After"*, and *"Journey to* Love" by **Connie Queen**, namely that self-love is the secret ingredient when it comes to igniting chains of miraculous moments. In fact, as experienced by **Sharon Gambrill** in her story *"A Miraculous Move"*, sometimes just finally believing yourself worthy is enough to set off the miraculous chain of events.

But the most important step is in allowing. And this is where is gets tricky for some. Because in order to allow miracles to occur we have to first develop the ability to identify what they look like. **Halina Kurowska** writes in *"Moments Of Grace"* that we so often dismiss miracles as coincidences, but more often than not these seemingly minor coincidences are in truth powerful divine synchronicities. As we learn in the chapter by **Donna Jutras Tobey**, *"All I Need is a Miracle"*, synchronicities are a part of the manifesting process and acting on them is paramount when it comes to bringing miracles into our experience. **Dr. Scott Ferriera** writes in his chapter *"A Divine Journey of the* Heart" of the importance of trusting in ourselves and in divine guidance, whatever form that takes. And sometimes, as chronicled in **Lisa Hardwick's** "Miraculous Messengers", that guidance can take its form in most surprising little manifestations indeed!

In my experience it is this trust that lets us fearlessly leap when opportunities arise. And they do arise, millions of times a day for everyone, regardless of their circumstance. It's not 'luck': it's a case of spotting the synchronicities, identifying them as signs of unformed miracles, and allowing ourselves to act to bring them into reality. And sometimes, as with **Deborah Bates** in her story *"Messenger of the Light"* it is *we* who are the real miracle.

This is simply how the divine operates. The chapter authored by **Katina Gillespie**, *"The Day My World Stopped"* may well be one of the most inspiring stories of divinity in operation I've ever read. It is truly a real life miracle story, from death to survival and from survival to rebirth. **Trish Bowie**, likewise, tells in her chapter "*Moving Beyond the Unknown*" about how the darkest and most harrowing tragedies can ignite the heart's journey towards miracle.

The reason it sometimes takes extreme sorrow and grief for miracles to show up is actually down to a common attribute of the human ego. Control. What does it take for us to relinquish control? How far can we push ourselves before we let the divine work through us? Embracing adversity with tenacity, patience and faith, as **Mimi Tran** demonstrated working on her aunt's farm as recounted in "*Believe in Yourself*", is also known as the Law of Non-Resistance. When you have released everything there is no longer a corresponding vibration within you to which adversity can attach itself.

But of course, nobody needs to wait for a tragedy to occur to bring miracles into their life. My own humble story points to a lifetime of miracles in action, although I have had my share of sorrow. Bullying at school led to a crisis of identity, which led to a decade of alcohol abuse, which led to plummeting self-esteem that didn't help when my best friend was killed in a car accident. But that's not the story I tell, I choose to talk about the blessings and successes that have been far more prevalent.

The actual reason *Manifesting Modern Miracles* is such a significant and powerful book lies in exactly that. These are *real* stories about *real* miracles experienced by *real* people as unique and evolving as you and I. In truth, the ability to manifest or allow miracles into our lives doesn't give us a free ticket to a lifetime without adversity. That's not what miracles are for. Life is duality, and it is in the contrasts of our experiences that we grow. But they do give us the tools to embrace that duality and to know when we're standing knee-deep in a terrible mess that the Infinite Wisdom, Power and Grace that created all things also knows how to fix this sticky situation. And we, created in the image of God, do too.

For this reason alone, rest assured: It'll all be alright in the end.

Elizabeth A. A. Wilson
http://www.eaawilson.com/

Tonia Browne

TONIA BROWNE is an author, teacher and coach. As a qualified teacher, Tonia has worked in the United Kingdom and internationally for over twenty years and was an Assistant Head for seven. She is a strong advocate of inviting fun into our lives and encouraging people to see their world from a different perspective. She can be contacted at:

Web URL: time4tblog.wordpress.com
Facebook: Time4T @ facebook.com/Time4Tonia
Twitter: twitter.com/ToniaUae

Minting Miracles: ABC Double Time

This chapter is to encourage you to become more aware of your perceptions. By doing so you have more clarity on what you are focusing on and hence through what type of lens you are seeing your world. You can then be more conscious about what you are doing so you can have more of the experiences you want. Included in this chapter is a memory aid to support you on your journey, hopefully as easy to use as ABC.

Minting Mess-Ups

"You look a bit down in the dumps. What's happened?" she asked.

"I've been dumped! Unceremoniously dumped!" I replied.

"You didn't really like him anyway, did you?"

"That's not the point and you know it!"

"Well, I've just been fired!"

"Oh no! Hang on, you hated your job!"

"I know, but that's not the point either, is it? It just doesn't feel good!"

"What a pair we are! We got rid of what we didn't want, but we haven't got what we do want. Where does that leave us?" I asked.

"I don't know! What's it all about? What's it all about?"

Minting Morse Codes

"It's just all too, too confusing, Alfie!" she said.

I was inclined to agree. How many times had we both got side-tracked from staying optimistic since we had known each other? We had tried to stay positive and focused. We had started many of the approaches suggested by numerous authors and coaches who advocated a better life. We achieved moments of success yet far more moments of wondering what was going on in our lives! I argued with her that we must be doing something right to have consciously manifested moments of happiness and success, even if it was only sometimes.

"Well, you're the teacher! Give me something easy to follow. I don't want a book. Give me a chapter. Do it for Alfie," she begged.

Alfie was our pseudonym for each other and also for all that was still unknown to us but that we wanted to understand. It came from the beautiful song *'Alfie'* about love being everything. We knew it from Cilla Black's rendition, but in the film by the same name it was sung by Cher. Michael Caine's famous line *'What's it all about, Alfie?'* became our catch phrase. I remembered the catch phrase from the film's intense last scene and my friend remembered it from the haunting song. This connection helped seal our friendship and we used these references in many of our conversations.

"Okay, we have nothing to lose. Let's try a fast-track yet simple approach then! We can call it Minting Miracles: ABC Double Time," I said, sounding much more confident than I felt.

Minting Metaphors

I knew the metaphor stating that the eyes are the windows to the soul. Yet more recently I came to understand that it's the eyes that are the windows through which the soul looks out into the world. This was a revelation to me, on-par with discovering that the tooth fairy came from the bedroom next door and not from outer space.

Instead of being examined by any Tom, Dick or Harry and analysed to our core as they peer into our souls, we have the power. It is we who are peering out into the world and analysing what we see, deciding what we like and what we do not. Yes, I still agree that by looking into the face of another you can see their feelings, especially if they're caught off guard. Yet what the newer meaning allows is more power. Instead of being vulnerable and transparent souls, we have more control to see our world and hence influence our reality more consciously. Once we understand this, we are better able to create phenomenal wonders.

Magnificent Moments

There is so much information available now, as well as a greater acceptance of spiritual topics and interest in self-development. Maybe it would be useful to present some of these complex ideas in a simplistic way. So I tried. I tried for the *Alfie* in all of us.

I believe the secret is to find the key that works for you. It is something we have to discover for ourselves. Yet, when we succeed, we often find that we are at the same door regardless of the journey. The key opens into a place of love, peace, happiness, service and possibilities. There are many places where you can find your key. If you have still misplaced yours, I encourage you to continue to search. I hope this approach gives you some clarity as to where to look and also encourages you to open the door when you get there.

MINTING MIRACLES: ABC DOUBLE TIME		
A is for	Asking	Accepting
B is for	Believing	Beginning
C is for	Committing	Continuing

Minting Messages: Ask and Accept

A is for being clear about what you are asking. It is also about accepting the signs that can help make it happen. I had not really appreciated the need for a conscious dialogue with the universe. Yes, I used to talk to myself, yet when I learnt to listen to how I spoke to myself I became aware that my words were not often uplifting and rarely motivating. *"You won't get that job. You're not that dynamic!"* I was telling the universe what I thought about myself and stating what would happen.

I was also not in the habit of accepting encouragement and support from other people. I didn't trust many people and felt I didn't need their help. I hadn't appreciated how controlling I was. I was closed to so many possibilities because of fear and I hid it behind a cloak called independence. I became more extravagant with my requests and more enthusiastic in my acceptance. I can ask for things specifically for myself or attributes to support my service to others. This didn't happen overnight. I had to adjust my self-perception to believe that I was worthy of asking and accepting better things to improve my life. Yet when I did, it was a win-win for me and for those around me.

SAY THE AFFIRMATION:

 I am happy to ask for and to accept good things in my life.

Minting Magic: Believe and Begin

B is for bringing trust back into your life so you can begin this approach to manifestation.

My belief that the universe had my back ended, if it ever started, about the same time I discovered the real face behind the Santa mask and the true identity of the tooth fairy. It can be difficult to begin taking action before you have trust, especially if you feel your earlier trust was misplaced. However, you need an element of this to begin the process that leads to the door to love, peace, happiness and possibility. Once you take those first few steps of action, however small they may be, you tell the universe you believe and changes can occur for you. It's not the other way around. You need an element of trust to ask and to accept. Trust and the consequential actions will result in shifts in your life.

SAY THE AFFIRMATION:

 I believe enough to begin believing for real. I take action now.

Minting Mystically: Commit and Continue

C is about not giving up. It is about staying focused and centred on your thinking and on your reactions and responses to life.

After you are willing to believe and take action on that belief, the advice is to commit to continue. It is easy to do this when there is instant proof it works. It can also be tempting to throw out the whole process if there is no proof manifesting soon enough for you. Yet this *Double C* is an important part of the process. Commit and continue with your asking and accepting and with believing and beginning. As with most things, manifestations need time to materialize. Don't get side-tracked from this strategy and allow self-doubt and negative self-talk to take centre stage again. If you persevere you will start to see changes in your life, as if by magic. You will also notice more miracles occurring.

I am often asked to explain miracle versus magic. My experience is that magic is more isolated and individualistic. It's a win or lose scenario, with you waiting for the outcome, whatever it may be. Magic is also what you can muster up using your own thinking and your own desires. Miracles are something altogether different and more amazing. They are not just about you. They are far bigger. Your journey may start with wanting things for yourself, then this desire for help moves on. Maybe you want help for your family or friends or for your workplace or for the environment. Wherever this desire goes, you will find a passion and your mission.

Once you commit and continue on this path, the momentum of magic magnifies beyond your expectations. You find that you have a new desire for service and miracles happen to help secure your success. When you are in the energy of miracles it is like a dance, a flow of helping and being helped. It involves wanting, asking, seeing, accepting, expressing gratitude, giving service, and so on, an endless loop. Miracles have a life of their own, often leading you to encourage and support others. As you do, it becomes an opportunity for you to hold up a key for others to take and to open the doors for themselves. Indeed, I now believe in the magic of the Santa mask and the tooth fairy all over again.

SAY THE AFFIRMATION:

 I commit and continue to create a better life.

Minting Mechanics

Once you are happy with accepting and encouraging the manifestation of miracles, you become more aware of the connection between us all. The more you help others the more it seems to help you.

My friend wanted to cut to the chase; to summarise some of the strategies we had read about. This *Minting Miracles: ABC Double Time* is what we discussed. It is a crib sheet to help you. It is by no means extensive and there is a lot more to this that you will discover. Yet it could be a key and if it fits, you are welcome to use it.

Minting Muses: Marriage and Music

Since the drama of the chapter's opening dialogue, a lot has happened. I was given further opportunities to analyse my relationships with others, myself and the world. As a consequence, I continued to ask for a new and happier way to live. I was not sure how that would manifest nor did I specify: a new business, a family focus or a move to a different geographic location. I was given signs that I accepted and before long I was indeed living a new and happier life.

One of the starting signposts of my journey was a series of synchronicities that introduced me to Patricia Crane and the Heal Your Life Workshops. These workshops, and the contacts I made through them, supported my amazing journey of self-development. When I allowed more love and trust into my life, new opportunities presented themselves. I am now married to a wonderful man and am focusing on writing to complement and support my passion for teaching and coaching. *Minting Miracles: ABC Double Time* worked for me, and I have a feeling that if she is open to this process my friend's life may turn out like the Broadway musical she wants it to be. Now that would be a double happy ending.

Manifesting Modern Miracles

MINTING MIRACLES: ABC DOUBLE TIME		
DOUBLE A	**Asking:** Be clear about your concept and the mechanics to get there	**Accepting:** Be aware of the signs and side-step the curve balls
DOUBLE B	**Believing:** Have trust that this works and keep that emotional connection open	**Beginning:** Take action and focus
DOUBLE C	**Committing:** Make this your priority with your energy and time	**Continuing:** This is an ongoing relationship: keep the courting going

"I like your ABC grid. It makes the process seem easy. You got your man. I will get my musical. It's Manifesting Modern Miracles in Double Time! Like Double ABC = Triple MMM!" she said with a smile.

"I am not sure about that! Remember, Minting Miracles: ABC Double Time is not a formula. It's a memory aid. I get the feeling miracles cannot be contained in a formula or in a time-frame. They just are. They are all places at all times."

"Very true and thank you. Alfie seems happy now and after all, that's what it's all about!"

Thank you to my mum and dad for giving me the miracle of life, to my friends who stuck by me whilst I made up my mind about what I wanted and to my amazing sister whose support and sense of humour means the world to me. A thank you also to the fabulous Lisa and her VIP team who have been amazing to work with, to Patricia Crane and the phenomenal speakers and authors I have encountered on my learning quest, and to my husband and best friend, who has helped me manifest many of my own modern day miracles.

Dedicated to the Alfie *in all of us. May* Alfie *continue to speak to you and motivate you. To all those who believed in me and supported me. To my family, to my friends and all the lovely people I have met and I am still to meet. To you if you are reading this book today and for those that will read it tomorrow: thank you and all the best.*

-Tonia Browne

Antoinette Coleman-Kelly

ANTOINETTE COLEMAN-KELLY from Ireland is an International

- Presenter and Transformative Life Coach
- "Heal Your Life" Facilitator, Coach and Business Trainer.

She is a lifelong Spiritual traveler with an inspiring, positive, vibrant and grateful outlook on life.

Antoinette is dedicated to motivating and inspiring people to discover change, achieve their dreams and reach their highest and best potential, working between Ireland and Boston USA.

www.lifehealing.ie
www.facebook.com/LifeHealingIre/

Stepping Delightfully Forward

Eleven years ago I was rendered emotionally, financially, spiritually and physically broken. Through all this, our boys were my prime concern. They were young and impressionable and not comprehending the logistics of life.

I had returned to college as a mature student to study Counselling and Psychotherapy (another challenge). A recurring thought was that there was no mistake at the timing of this heartache. There is a saying *"Everything happens for a reason."* Well, I didn't quite get the reason and yet I was supported greatly with family, friends and colleagues.

My world had quite literally shattered on 13th December, and yes, so close to Christmas. He announced he wanted out of our union. In total shock, I remember standing in the kitchen that fateful evening and thinking, "Oh my God... Can this really be happening? What money do I have? Are the Boys okay?"

The Cacophony in my head was alarming. I believe I went on autopilot mode, not only for that Christmas, yet for a very long time, years in fact. I learned and pulled on every skill I possessed, and indeed on many skills that I hadn't realised that I had, many acquired long before my nursing days!

It's amazing where often when we believe our mistakes or events are unfixable, actually, they are the learning curves for the present moment. Life often imposes things on you that you have no control, and I know I have a choice on how I'm going to live through this.

One thing I knew for sure that evening was that I *would* survive this. After all, I *had* survived life up to this moment. I did not understand the *how* and yet I had the 'knowing' I could overcome this, too.

I have always believed that God does not give you something that you cannot deal with. This was a life lesson with its own platform.

I remember thinking that evening that I would not touch alcohol as I felt if I had one glass, I might not be able to stop; such was the pain and devastation I felt. Actually I didn't take a glass for several years.

The knowledge that you only have yourself to rely on is very empowering and in those early days, it was important simply to focus on breathing and repeating the mantra:

I remember putting coloured post-it notes with "Breathe" on them all over the house. The staircase, the kitchen, the fridge, the bathroom, every door in the house got decorated with post-it notes reminding me to continue breathing.

I began writing and writing and writing. I wrote about what was going on in my head and my body. I didn't just write lines and pages, I wrote forests and then I enthusiastically burnt every single page.

It is always good to remember, when you write like this, refrain from re-reading your script. As you write, it is never a good idea to re-read the page. You have just managed to get it out of your system, do not internalise it again. I find, for me personally, the writing is a great release as it is often difficult to verbalise your deeper inner feelings.

I often joke, that when I write, "I can often use language that I am too much of a lady to pronounce!"

There is massive healing in the burning of these written pages. Burning them in a sink and then flushing them away under running water is akin to healing, as we clear all away with the dead ashes.

On one particular evening, the struggle was unbearable. I was writing multiple pages and so intent on burning those at the kitchen sink, that I almost set the kitchen alight. Such was my determination to be rid of my internal dialogue. Thankfully the kitchen survived and oh, by the way, I did too.

Soon afterwards there came the news that there was going to be a new-born in his life. This added to the volumes of writing and the use of reams of paper. I wondered if I needed to plant some trees or even a forest as I may soon run out of paper!

Today our boys are amazing young men and the two younger children are delightful weekend visitors with lots of fun, joy and laughter.

My passion today has come from overcoming many adversities, gingerly, gracefully and successfully rising to each challenge. I strongly believe in "being better, not bitter".

My ability to forgive is paramount on this phenomenal journey. Louise L Hay says that *"forgiveness does not condone someone else's poor behavior; it means letting go of our stuff on the situation."* As we learn to forgive, it is important to forgive ourselves, too. Forgiveness is truly a real gift to ourselves.

I believe I am writing this as a declaration. I'm declaring that I do not want to live my life in regret. I declare and that I am taking my life delightfully forward, affirming what I do want in my life. This is about not letting life slip through my fingers, it's about seizing the day.

It's about finding ways to get over, go under, go around and through the obstacles to find life's treasures.

Follow your dreams and enjoy being spontaneous, live and love your best self.

As I step delightfully forward with passion I feel vibrant and strong, and my light is shining brightly. I am grateful for the lessons along the way as I receive this modern miracle.

I have learned to truly say "Thank You."

STEPPING DELIGHTFULLY FORWARD

Hard to believe it's been 28 years
With a friend like you
To stand by me, hold my hand
And help us through thick and thin

It's been up and down
We've had our share of both
Facing obstacles and miracles together
As life moves on and on

Enjoying much laughter
Awesome days, weeks, months and years
You knew me so well
And I thank you for all of that

WE were meant to connect
Our life it's been fabulous
I'm proud to be your friend
And that you are our boys amazing DAD

May our lives be bountiful?
And keeping our dreams alive
AS a Mum and Dad
Let's keep stepping delightfully forward.

-ANTOINETTE COLEMAN-KELLY

Awesome gratitude to my family and
Friends for their unconditional love and support.
In Memory of my Amazing Mum and Dad.

To the amazing Lisa Hardwick and
Visionary Insight Press – Thank You.

To my many enlightened teachers and
mentors around the world – Deep Gratitude.

-Antoinette Coleman-Kelly

Katina F Gillespie

KATINA F GILLESPIE is trained, certified, and licensed as a Peace Love Wings, Mind Body Spirit Practitioner and Workshop Facilitator, Project Director at Visionary Insight Press and active volunteer with Women's Resource Center of Manatee.

Katina grew up on a farm in central Illinois, completed a Bachelor of Science in Psychology from the University of Memphis, and has lived in southeast Florida, Baltimore Maryland, Central Florida and now resides in Southwest Florida with her life partner Charles, her dog Kiwi, and cat Karma.

She has an extensive background in restaurant and hotel management. She worked in several cities and various restaurants/hotels at many levels. Katina returned to her calling of assisting others and created Emotional Harmony and Wellness so that she may encourage others to acknowledge and promote their best self and communicate their inner wisdom.

www.EmotionalHarmonyWellness.com
katina@emotionalharmonywellness.com
www.facebook.com/emotionalharmonywellness/

 The Day My World Stopped

One moment I was enjoying the wind rush through my hair, the next moment, I was shaking hands with the grim reaper in a roadside ditch! I was seventeen years old and had been in a motorcycle accident as a passenger. I was declared dead on the scene as I had no pulse or brain activity. They were able to find a weak pulse by the time the ambulance arrived to the emergency room. I was dead for approximately 15 minutes. This was the beginning of a VERY long and painful journey that continues to linger in every new chapter of my life that unfolds.

I was not wearing a helmet and landed directly on my head at approximately 70 miles an hour. I had global brain damage but the majority of the hemorrhaging and injury was in my frontal lobe where my brain had been pushed against my skull on impact. I had a bruise on my hip where my body landed after the initial impact. I only weighed 110 pounds and was athletic and fit. Your frontal lobe controls your emotions and your memory. When I woke after being in a comma for five days, I was a blank slate. I showed no emotion and what I felt, I did not understand. I had total amnesia and had no clue who I was or anything about my past. After six weeks in the hospital learning basic faculties such as walking, eating, and bathing. I was scheduled to be released. The prognosis was grim. I was told that I would be lucky to graduate high school and that I would NOT be able to get a college education. I would never be able to cheer again and my basic faculties would not return to normal. I was basically told that with the amount of brain damage that I incurred I would be on government assistance for the remainder of my life and be unable to care for myself.

Although I was not able to comprehend the full extent to what I was being told I did not think that those were viable options. I immediately started to prove the doctors wrong. I was working with a physical therapist, acupuncturist, pain specialist, and a chiropractor so that we could allow my neck to have full range of motion. It took about six months for that to happen. My psychiatrist and neurologist had me on a cocktail of psyche meds and pain medicine. My psychologist was doing his best to determine what I was capable of accomplishing. Keeping track of my doctor visits was a full time job. I had a calendar and a journal to track everything.

I was determined to graduate high school on time and with my class of 1992. So my mother made arrangements for a tutor to come out to the family farm so that I could complete my classes I was unable to finish my junior year. I was not released to cheer my senior year so I coached the freshman team. I truly loved being a coach! I would meet them early in the morning for practice before the summer heat set in. I then had physical therapy, tutor, chiropractor, or other doctor appointments every day after practice. I was not about to let these things slow me down. I had not been released to drive yet so my mother, God bless her, had to drive me EVERY where. She was happy to do it and didn't want to let me out of her sight for a moment since we were not certain of how I may react physically or mentally to any situation. I was bi-polar, very confused and in a great deal of pain both physically and mentally.

I was able to pass the classes I needed to in order to start my senior year with the rest of my classmates. I attended normal classes but I was unable to transfer information from short term to long term memory. I had to tape record all of the classes and listen to them later to fill in the empty spaces in my notes. Most of the information I was learning for the first time. For example, I didn't know what the constitution or Bill of Rights were. My teachers were amazing and very patient as I would meet with them after class and ask MANY questions. I did not tell my friends about the difficulties I was experiencing. Actually, I had very few friends my senior year. They all turned their backs on me and walked away after I was released from the hospital.

Teenagers have two defense mechanisms. Fight or Flight. They did not understand what they were fighting so they chose flight. I was a social butterfly prior to the accident and now I only had my family. When I would go to school I had my teachers and an occasional boyfriend that was only concerned with what I could do for him physically. I do not want to come across ungrateful. I have the most amazing support system in my family. Their love has no boundaries.

Since I did not have friends in high school, I turned to friends at the local university. I started practicing with the college cheer team. I was determined to cheer again!!! I picked up a full time job at Subway and I hired a body building trainer. I wanted to be in the best shape possible so that I would be able to make the cheer team my freshman year in college. I became obsessed! I was weight and cardio training six days a week. I even competed for the first 'American Gladiators'. I was down to less than 9% body fat. I graduated high school with honors! I was accepted to the local university and I made the college Junior Varsity Cheer team! I did three things that I was told I couldn't in less than two years after the accident. I was super proud of my accomplishments but had very few people to share them.

There were however, a couple of bumps in the road. I mentioned that I was on a number of psychiatric medications. I lost my sense of smell due to my olfactory nerve being severed. With that, I cannot taste many things, as most of the flavor of food/beverage is in the scent of it. I had not experimented with adult beverages much prior to the accident. But I sure did AFTER. I was unaware of how to get people to talk with me since most of my friends wanted nothing to do with me. So I turned to alcohol. Granted, this is the WORST thing I could have done considering the amount of medication that I was taking combined with the brain damage. One night I heard a tap on my bedroom window. It was some 'friends' of mine that wanted to surprise me. I was super excited to see them! Their surprise was a friend of mine who had moved away and was visiting. The four of us went out drinking. I had previously dated one of them. He decided that he wanted me to drive him home. So they brought me back to my house and we picked up my car. He decides to have sex with me and then degrade me and tell me what I whore I am. He had me drop him off at his parents' house and I drove away in hysterical tears! I decided not to drive home. I turned the other direction and ended up driving my car off a bridge. It was the same road that my motorcycle accident was on 18 months earlier AND the same officer on the scene. This time I was unconscious in my car that was on its side after rolling down the embankment of the bridge. I had a .38 Blood Alcohol Level. .08 is the legal limit and .4 you are considered dead. I do not recall actually driving OFF the bridge but I vividly recall how I felt the next day. I was ANGRY. It was the first time I understood my emotions. I was angry and frustrated because I was alive. There is nothing I wanted more than to be dead! "Why can't God just let me die?" I asked my parents repeatedly. I was laying on the couch at their house and they would take turns sitting next to me and all they would say is *"I LOVE you"*. It's the best thing they could do. I mean what does a parent say to their eighteen-year-old daughter that wants to die?

This was the beginning of many struggles and much therapy. Outwardly, I was a great actress. I kept my battles private. I felt the local community hated me. They were angry because they worried about me when I was in the hospital and I looked fine when I was released. I was not crippled or mangled so they believed there were no 'real' injuries. My family must have made up everything! I continued to check off all of the things that I was told I couldn't do and ignored what I was really feeling for the most part. I took the psychiatric medication prescribed which basically added to my blank stare. It took away any emotion I may have had because the last thing a psychiatrist wants is for his/her patient to FEEL. If the patient feels emotion, then they no longer have a client and believe me, they took FULL advantage of my parent's medical insurance. I needed the medication for maybe the first year, but was kept on it for four.

I matriculated at the local college where I was on the cheer team, voted into student government, eighteen credit hours of classes, full time job, working out, tutors, continued therapy and an active social life. Somehow, I was able to fit 28 hours into each day. I did not require much sleep. I had accomplished many things for the student body in my short time involved with the student government so I decided to run for student body president. I had put together a party called REALITY. The slogan was "It's all talk unless YOU make it happen". The party consisted of representatives of a wide variety of organizations. I was very proud of the diversity and each candidate's commitment to improving student life. The opposing party was only represented by Social Greek Fraternities and Sororities. I am not opposed to these organizations but you would never find me as a member of a social Greek organization. I was a member of a number of Academic Fraternities but not social. Anyway, in order to be on the opposing party you must be a member of the Greek community or pledging to be in one. I found out that one of my friends that I went to high school with, who I was on the cheer team with in high school was a member of this party. She was 'rushing' one of the sororities. I later found out that she had told the school paper about my attempted suicide to discredit my integrity and stability. It was printed and I was HORRIFIED!!! I did not make a formal response. I refused to stoop to her level and the other party's level. I simply acted like it was not there but privately met with the members of my party to explain the circumstance in the event they were questioned or had questions themselves. The election happened and the ballots were cast. We found out the day of election that the individuals who were 'rushing' the Greek houses were told to stuff 50 ballots each if they wanted a seat in the Greek house. A form of hazing, if you will, to prove their desire to be a part of the social organization.

One of the things that I did prior to running for Student Body President was assist in reviewing and re-writing the student government constitution. After the results of the election were tallied and the opposing party won every spot by approximately the same number of votes. We asked for a re-count of the ballots. Conveniently, the person in charge of student government also was the faculty member that was in charge of the Greek governing body. The ballots were shredded immediately after they were counted. This was against the Student Government Constitution. The ballots were to be kept for a minimum amount of time following the election in the event there was any foul play or fraud. I asked for a meeting with the VP of Student Affairs and the President of the University. The VP's wife was one of my teacher's in high school and I was the only student on the panel of faculty who chose the university's new president. He also went to the same church as my family. I knew them both outside of their professional rolls. In the meeting I requested the university to hold another election due to the fraud and violation of the constitution. I would NOT be running for Student Body President since I was the one suggesting the re-election, but felt the students deserved an honest election.

They refused my request. I was expecting them to. I looked at them both in the eye and asked "Would you risk the integrity of this university to save its reputation?" Both of them replied YES. I excused myself, walked down the hall to admissions, and withdrew from the university. I have not set foot on the campus since that day.

After this happened I decided to move to Memphis to study with a professor that my psychologist had told me about. He was one of the founding psychologist of neuropsychology and specialized in head injuries and specifically rehabilitation after head injury. I had changed my major from Elementary Education to Psychology. I wanted to work with other head injured individuals and help them understand therapy and recovery. I wanted to let them know that IT IS POSSIBLE! Take out all of the negative diagnosis that I had been given. I lived in Memphis for a year before starting classes so that I could establish residency and pay in-state tuition. One day during this transition, I decided to stop ALL the medication. I DO NOT recommend this! I repeat, I DO NOT recommend this. It can be very dangerous! I took all of my meds and flushed them down the toilet. I decided that I didn't like the way they made me feel and how they controlled me. Granted, I was on medication for bi-polar disorder, depression, hallucinations, and pain. I was also drinking alcohol, marijuana, and occasional cocaine with these medications. Not a good combination by any account. Stopping the medication ended up being very good for me. I pulled up my boot straps, if you will, and found my inner strength. I stopped all of my therapy, started school and graduated with a Bachelor of Science in Psychology, concentration of neuropsychology and a minor in women's studies. I was accepted into Emory University in Atlanta for their Neuropsychology Graduate Program. I decided to get married and allow my husband to get his degree with the intention that I would attend Graduate School when he finished. When in reality I was afraid of failing and did not have the confidence to go to Graduate School and my husband was a great 'reason' to get out of trying that no one would question.

I did not realize many of this as it was happening or at least I did not mentally acknowledge the actual emotions attached. I was going through the motions and remember only snap shots. It's mostly a blur. It took me 20 years to realize that others were unaware of how they damaged me or I should say how I ALLOWED them to damage me. They only did what they knew how. I was taking it personally and most of them had long forgotten about ME. I realized that it was my choice to hold on to the emptiness, pain, hurt, anger, and betrayal OR I could let it go, forgive and start living. There were many emotional scars and walls that developed due to the events following the accident. The pain and physical rehab took a little over two years to heal. The physical damage in itself is a miracle that I survived. I am reminded of every time I see a new neurologist. They review my brain scans, look at me and say "you should not be able to hold a conversation or remember the conversation with the amount damage and location". I'm missing about a quarter of my frontal lobe, bilateral damage.

The emotional and psychological torment is what I allowed to follow for many years and to this day creeps up every now and again. My lesson through it all... 90 percent of your worries/concerns are fabricated in your mind. 10 percent are real. Only YOU have the choice of how to react to any given situation. Bad things happen to good people all the time! How are YOU going to react? The happiness of your life depends on the quality of your thoughts. If you believe you are going to fail, you will. Challenges promote, increase, and strengthen your highest self if you allow them. Choosing to concentrate on what you need to improve and what you consider failure will only promote more failure. As you choose to concentrate on strengths, more strength and forward motion will occur.

I have been deemed a "Miracle" on many occasions. I do believe in the power of prayer and intention. Call it whatever you feel comfortable with and what best fits your mindset, value and belief system. My family and community/tribe believed in the power of prayer and used their fellowship to send positive intention and belief when I was in the hospital and in need of encouragement. Other times I have decided to change my perspective and it changes the outcome. The power of positive thought. Place the credit where you wish but the bottom line is that if YOU believe you achieve! You were never created to live depressed, guilty, condemned, ashamed or unworthy. You were created to be victorious and a success! I decided that I would not be a victim or at least I thought I did. I did all of the things that I was told that I would never be able to physically accomplish. Outwardly I was a hero! The true miracle occurred when I chose to stop feeling hurt, betrayed, and a victim of emotional torment. My life completely opened when I chose love, pride, and gratitude. I replaced all of the negative emotions with those of positive value that allows me to move onward and upward to heights I never imagined and with the grounding to back it up. I will not fall again for I have a foundation of trust and belief in ME and that my friends cannot be broken!

It's time to manifest YOUR miracle!

Dedicated to my mother, Judy, for her dedication and devotion to me during my most difficult battle - because of you I know and love myself more freely. And to my best friend and partner in life, Charles, for your unconditional love and support. The Light in my heart continues to shine brighter with you by my side.

A tremendous debt of gratitude to all coaches, teachers and students of life who continue to welcome me in their paths and provide me with inspiration, understanding and opportunities for growth. I am grateful for all of the wonderful family members and friends that allow the love from the Universe to flow abundantly in our lives. Namaste!

~ Katina F Gillespie

Lisa Hardwick

Many believe that they were blessed when the Universe led them directly to Lisa Hardwick to assist them with the roadmap to living their life's purpose.

Lisa is fiercely committed to guiding Spiritual Entrepreneurs to achieve their dream of becoming a published author, to help them build a strong network and to assist them with a plan that works so they can make an abundant living doing what they are passionate about. If you're looking for a proven professional who can guide you to Develop an Action Plan of everything you will need to succeed and create financial energy as a Spiritual Entrepreneur, then you've come to the right place. With many years of experience working with clients and guiding them to achieve remarkable successes, her mission is to share valuable tools and resources so you can make an actual living as a Spiritual Entrepreneur. If you're ready to answer the call and align with your passion by taking the simple steps to make it your life's work, then connect with Lisa today to set up an initial consultation.

To learn more about Lisa, please visit: www.lisahardwick.com.

Miraculous Messengers

I'd just left my hair stylist. I got in my car, started it up — and that's when I felt it. That feeling of "knowing" that I was surrounded by the loving energy of those who had ascended before me — the ladies that had been in my life almost my entire existence — my grandmothers, great grandmothers, great aunts.

In the most miraculous ways, their energy shows up to guide me. They let me know that everything's okay. That it's all working perfectly, that I'm safe and protected and I just need to trust the process.

And once in a while, they give me a physical sign — a ladybug.

As I pulled out onto the cobblestone road, I thought about calling a friend whom I hadn't connected with in months. I wanted to see if she'd like to meet for coffee at our favorite place. I turned the corner and there she was!

"Wow!" I said out-loud. And then that's when it happened. A ladybug landed on my windshield directly in front of me.

Every time this happens, I cry tears of joy. Not big tears, just those small sweet ones that make your eyes really watery and cause a thin single tear or two to trickle down your face. You know the kind — right?

My wonderful spirit guides were just letting me know they were there; that there was more to this life than most people understand. And I had the tear stain to prove it.

Another time I was in Florida with my friend Lisa, a wonderful artist who goes by the name, "Chicago Mermaid." We were laying by the pool, reading and enjoying the sun when once again I felt this beautiful energy surround me. It was as if this force was enhancing my enjoyment of the present moment. I felt so good — like I was floating on a heavenly cloud.

I set down my book and turned onto my back and shut my eyes. I let the sun wash over my body and just reveled in the "Now." It felt incredible. Like everything in my life was perfect.

Suddenly, something landed on my cheek, startling me and pulling me out of my bliss-filled state. I picked it off lightly and quickly sat up. It took a while for my eyes to adjust because of the blinding sun reflecting off the pool. Yet even before looking, I had a "knowing" of what was in my hand.

You guessed it. It was a ladybug.

Lisa smiled. Not only had we not seen a ladybug in the couple of weeks we'd been in Florida, we'd not seen even one bug. But, there it was, giving me a sign that those wonderful ladies were supporting me, guiding me and letting me know I was exactly where I was supposed to be.

Sometimes, their energy draws me elsewhere to make their presence known. Like the time I was in my kitchen and felt an urging — an intuitive feeling — to go to the garage.

My day had been challenging. I was feeling a little overwhelmed with the project I'd been working on. I actually thought, "Jeesh, I really don't have time for this right now." Yet, I knew by then I had to follow my impulses.

I was drawn to some bricks leftover from a landscaping project that my husband and I had done the previous weekend. I smiled as I reminisced how my son came to help us lay the bricks. I remembered how it started to rain — yet we just kept going — sliding in the mud, hurrying as fast as we could. We laughed at how silly the neighbors must have thought we were to be working in our yard in the middle of a downpour. Good times.

I felt moved to pick up one of the bricks. I had this thought that maybe I was being inspired to create something out of it; perhaps use it as a canvas to paint on, like my cousin does.

Then I looked down at the spot where I'd just removed the brick. Right in the center of the brick below was a ladybug. I gently touched the little bug with one finger and just kept saying, "Thank you, thank you, thank you … " over and over. I'm being guided and supported. Everything is going to be okay. I'm right were I'm supposed to be. Oh, how I needed that sign on that day!

All of us are given signs that we're being guided and supported by divine love. There are many different names for this force — which is not of this world — and it seems that those of us who have the "knowing," are the ones who experience it.

I've always been a very intuitive person. Even as a child I felt it, even though I didn't know what to call it. I just thought I was different than everyone else. Now I know what a gift it is and I'm extremely grateful.

Don't you think it would be wonderful to have beings pop into your life every so often just to let you know that they've got your back? Let me tell you, it is. Signs are all around but often people miss them. I learned of my ladybug sign years ago during a guided meditation.

Would you like to know what your sign is from the holy divine? Just read the following meditation and your personal sign will be revealed at the end.

By the way, there are many meditation scripts available for asking this, or any question, of the divine; I chose this one because it's one of my favorites that I've written and it takes place on a beach. And if you know me, you know how much I love the beach!

So just sit back and relax. There's no reason to close your eyes, unless you want to. And in that case, either record and play the meditation, or have someone read the words to you. There's no right or wrong way to do this.

First, take some long, deep, cleansing breaths to relax your body.

Imagine standing upon the shore of a beautiful tropical island. As you gaze out to sea, you notice the most brilliant turquoise hues of water blending with deep shades of cobalt blue. The waves are gently lapping along the shoreline. Underneath your feet, the sand feels like silk, as you slowly walk along the beach.

Several feet in front of you, you notice something shiny, glistening in the sun. Moving closer, you see that it's a bottle. You pick it up. There's a piece of rolled-up paper inside. Removing the cork, you take out the scroll and unfurl it. It's a treasure map!

You realize it's a map of the island you're standing on. Curious, you trace the lines on the map to a drawing of a palm tree. You lift your gaze. Straight ahead, you see the very same palm tree a short distance away.

Moving swiftly now, you come to the same exact point on the beach where there's an "X" illustrated on the map. Filled with anticipation, you dig through the soft sand.

Several inches below the surface, you discover an old wooden box. You free it from the earth's grasp and brush off the sand. This is no ordinary box. This is a treasure chest!

Sitting back on your heels, you fervently open the ancient box. There's a scroll inside. The paper and markings appear to be identical to the earlier one you found. Hastily, you unroll it and read the message scrawled across the page: "Herein lies the answers that your soul seeks regarding your sign from the divine."

Gleefully, you rummage through the chest. Your hand closes around something unfamiliar. You take a deep breath. You have a "knowing" that whatever it is, it's your sign from the holy divine.

You bring it closer for a better look. You smile as you speak aloud what you are holding.

So there you go. Now you know what your sign is. Don't question it — it is what it is. And whenever you see this object, number, letter, or whatever you "saw" during the meditation, your own sign from the divine, you'll now have a "knowing" that you're guided and supported.

I just love this for you!

We can all learn the answers to any questions we have. We can connect any time we want to those who have transitioned and ask for help through different forms of prayer or meditation. Prayer is when we speak to the divine, whereas meditation is when we listen to it. Put the two together and it's really powerful.

I enjoy sharing and teaching guided imagery meditations at the writers' workshops I facilitate. There's something special about watching others relax and receive messages to assist them with their healing. Simply beautiful.

Recently, I was in Arizona hosting "Meet and Greets" for writers in various cities. While in Sedona, a dear friend of mine, Deb Power, and I decided to climb the "big rock" at Red Rock State Park. We affirmed we would make it all the way to the top.

It was really hot that day. We were already pretty warm when we got out of the Jeep in the parking lot. While Deb opened the Jeep's tailgate to get us some bottled water, I unfolded the map to determine where we were supposed to go.

And then it happened.

A ladybug dropped right onto the center of the map. Right dab in the middle. I let out some kind of sound. I can't remember what it was, but it got Deb's attention and she came running around the side of the vehicle.

She looked down at the ladybug and then questioned me with her eyes. I whispered, "It's just as if it dropped out of the sky."

Then it flew away as quickly as it showed up. The tears of joy began, filling my eyes. Deb hugged me tightly. Like most of my close friends, she knew the ladybug was my sign. Now you know, too. I guess that makes you one of my close friends, too. Awesome!

As Deb and I sauntered towards the "big rock" we talked about her sign from her parents who have transitioned — a hummingbird. I thought how I should get Deb something with a hummingbird on it as a souvenir before we leave Arizona. We walked around a building to get on the trail to the rock and as we did we were greeted by some beautiful birds.

Hummingbirds!

Dedicated to Lisa Donahue (aka: Chicago Mermaid) and to Deb Power. Both of you have been there to witness such incredible miracles with me and that is just one of the many reasons I hold a very special place in my heart for each of you. May your days be filled with an abundance of dimes, pears and hummingbirds.

I would like to acknowledge Leonie Dawson, Katina Gillespie, Brenda Fedorchuk, Nate Graham, Chelle Thompson, Wendy Kitts, Elizabeth Andrzejewski Wilson, Lance Wallace and Kim Scott for their incredible devotion and/or guidance to the Visionary Insight Press team. The tenacity and talent each of you share assists with raising the vibration of every person we have the pleasure of being of service to.

-Lisa Hardwick

Halina Kurowska

HALINA KUROWSKA is an author, writer, speaker, personal mentor, licensed Heal Your Life® teacher and Life Coach. She holds an Honours Bachelor of Arts degree in Philosophy from the University of Toronto.

Halina has spent the last twenty-five years on a path of spiritual development. Having transcend her own life, she is now assisting others in their transformation. Halina's unique insight based on extensive studies of spiritual wisdom and its application in her own life, allows her to help others get in touch with their own inner wisdom. She lovingly empowers people and leads them to joy through her workshops and coaching sessions at Living with AWE: Awareness, Wisdom, Empowerment.

Halina is a happy and proud mother of two amazing sons, Wit and Mateusz, grateful to them for sharing this lifetime and their teachings with her.

Halina loves nature, hiking, practicing meditation, reading, writing and travelling.

www.livingwithawe.com
halina@livingwithawe.com
www.facebook.com/livingwithawe/

Moments of Grace

"The whole world is a series of miracles, but we're so used to seeing them that we call them ordinary things."

~ HANS CHRISTIAN ANDERSEN

We all encounter miracles in our daily lives, but, trained to rely on the logical side of our brain, we do not always recognize them. We do not pay attention to the wonder unfolding in front of us and we dismiss miraculous occurrences as coincidence or wave them off as insignificant. At times, even profound moments of grace go unnoticed, unrecognized for their greatness, filed under 'oh, that just happened like that.'

Since the nature of life itself is miraculous, I've come to believe that everything in life is a miracle. I know that miracles are all around us, we just have to open our eyes and hearts to notice them. *A Course In Miracles*, a self-taught form of spiritual psychotherapy, states that miracles are natural. They are the effect of our alignment with the Universal Intelligence, which is Love and Truth. Miracles occur when the invisible and infinite possibilities unfold as realities in our lives. They are a universal blessing to us all.

I have been blessed in my life with some awe-inspiring mystical experiences, but here I want to share with you the everyday miracles that have changed my life. My goal is to show you that miracles are all around, we just need to notice them. It is important that we periodically stop and remind ourselves about the wonder of it all — the wonder that we call life.

My year of miracles started, as miracles usually do, with disappointment. It was a beautiful summer day as I set off to work. Before me, lay a day full of visiting moms with babies. This had been my job now for fifteen years and I loved many aspects of it. While I was basically tasked with providing guidance and information about babies, I offered these women so much more. Many visits would start with a woman crying, overwhelmed by her new responsibilities and unsure about her future. By sharing my story and the tools I used to lift myself up, I offered them hope for a better tomorrow, inspiration to start doing things to make life better and easier, and, most important, I restored their belief in themselves and in the good that is in the world. Each of my visits was a mission to make this world a better place, more kind and loving.

I had four visits scheduled for that day. As I completed them, one by one, sharing love and kindness with each of them, I was filled with even more love and a deep satisfaction with what I do. It is very rewarding to be able to touch people's lives in such a deep and, hopefully, lasting way. Each visit that day ended with hugs: children and moms hug me, happy, hopeful, smiling, knowing that there is good in the world. During my last visit, I received a phone call from my manager asking me to come to the office right away. I drove back wondering what was going on. I didn't have to wait long to get my answer: "You are fired!"

Hearing those words did not make me angry, just very sad, confused and scared. I could not understand why this decision had been made and how someone could deliver it with such insensitivity. But, most important, I was frightened about my future. At the age of fifty-four, I suddenly found myself unemployed. No job security, no safety blanket. What was I going to do?

I sat at home with my sweet cat, Charlotte, stroking her soft fur and crying. "What will we do now," I asked her. Charlotte's purring provided little comfort as my mind kept going back to the same thought: I have no idea what to do next. I have no plan whatsoever.

I didn't know it at the time, of course, but this critical time in my life was actually a moment of grace. It didn't feel like it at the time, but it was, nonetheless, exactly what I was seeking.

For years now, I had been wanting to parlay those fleeting moments of joy I felt at imparting knowledge and joy to a new mother into a full-time career as a spiritual counsellor. I knew there was training available for this type of work — and I often dreamt about getting a license to do it — but I never had the time. About a month after I got fired, an email popped into my inbox from Heal Your Life. Although I had been signed up for these emails for quite a while, never before had I received one regarding training. It said that only two spots remained in a training course to become a Heal Your Life Counsellor. This was the training I had been dreaming of and now, fired from my job, I actually had the time to do it.

I sent an email asking them to hold a spot for me. My journey towards a new career had begun.

The training in San Diego was much more emotionally intense than I could have imagined. It was a coming together of souls, a gathering of a tribe. Instant soul recognition, closeness and love was shared. Even in the week leading to this training, while preparing for the trip, I already felt closeness to those who were also preparing to go — even though I had never met them before. Scenes from the movie '*Close Encounters of the Third Kind,*' came flashing to my mind often during that week and I felt as if I was preparing for an important journey of the Soul ready to meet my soul-family. Deep in my heart I felt and knew that it was the voice of my Soul that led me during that time. Overwhelming feelings of love, gratitude, wonder and surrender to the rhythm of life were my constant companion during those days.

Immersed in the beauty of my surroundings, I embraced the teachings and people who shared this time and space with me. Our soul connections were truly beyond ordinary words, they were sweeping and deep. In some instances, the feeling of knowing the person already was truly undeniable, yet we had never met in this lifetime before. It was a magical time, with like-minded and like-hearted people sharing their common vision and love with each other.

It was during that time that I started to hear about publishing opportunities. I had, for a long time, entertained the idea of writing professionally. During my time of unemployment, when I was searching for my next step, I had run into an old acquaintance of mine. I shared with her my recent disappointments and my secret desire to publish my work. I said, "I've always loved writing. I write in my journal all the time." Her response was a classic one of someone who believes in limitations imposed on us through social conditioning. "That's not easy, impossible almost," she insisted. "Getting published, even self-published, is extremely difficult and there is lots of competition out there." Needless to say, I felt discouraged and shooed those ideas out of my mind. But in San Diego, surrounded by a group of positive and like-minded souls, my mind started to open to the realness of this possibility.

About a month after the training was completed, the opportunity to write came knocking. Totally by chance, an email from a publisher appeared in my inbox. She later revealed she had accidentally pressed 'send to all' on her mailing list. She had never intended to invite everyone to participate in this project. My inbox flashed with a message: "If you are interested in participating in our next compilation book *Whispers of the Heart*, sign up!" What do I do now, I thought frantically and excitedly? As with any big decision, I decided to sleep on it. Asking for guidance, I went to sleep. In the morning, I awoke with an answer: If I don't do this now, I will regret it. With a trembling heart, I signed up.

It was Christmastime and my family was absorbed in watching TV while I was reading my email. A message popped up from my publisher announcing the tag line for *Whispers of the Heart*. It was: '*Today's most inspirational teachers, healers and spiritual leaders share their stories of following the voice of their wise inner being and the impact it made in their lives.*' My heart trembled with elation and joyful tears filled my eyes. I felt like I had finally been recognized for my true self — I am a healer, a spiritual counsellor and a teacher of LOVE. With my family close by and my heart filled with gratitude, I sat down in the dying days of 2014 to write the first words of my chapter for the book.

In those moments, when I thought about being a writer and becoming a published author, I felt what Louise Hay calls 'an inner ding.' I call it simply my inner guide. This feels like your heart jumps with joy, sometimes slightly and, at times, it trembles with excitement and uncertainty. You are exhilarated and scared at the same time. My heart was overwhelmed with immense amounts of gratitude as I've realized that it was more than writing a chapter for the book. I was writing a new chapter of my life.

In the days following the loss of my job, I had no specific plan as to what I wanted to do next. I knew my dreams, yet had no idea how to go after them. I only knew deep within my heart that I wanted my life to unfold in the most miraculous way possible. So even during that foggy period of my life, I was totally open and trusting, surrendering to the divine guidance of the Universe. At that time, I had reached out to my dear friend Magda, who is an artist and lives her life free of society's constraints. At 81 years old, she is full of enthusiasm, curiosity and wisdom. On the phone, when she asked me what I was going to do, I said, "I want to be like you. A free spirit."

So, a year to the day my life came crashing down around me, I assessed my life and realized that I had fulfilled most of my secret hopes and aspirations. I am a Licensed Heal Your Life Teacher and Life Coach, founder of 'Living with AWE: Awareness, Wisdom, Empowerment,' and a twice-published author.

Some may call what happened to me during that year a series of coincidences. But I will say this: there are no coincidences in life, only synchronicities that are orchestrated by the great Universal Intelligence that governs all nature and manifests itself through our intuitive wisdom. There are a few definitions of what constitutes a miracle and one is to view it as anything that redirects the events of our lives to something better. The things that we only dared wish for quietly in our hearts, materialize in front of us and become our lives. These are the ordinary, everyday miracles that come to us when we choose love, gratitude and forgiveness.

A Course In Miracles defines a miracle as a shift in perception from fear to love. As Marianne Williamson, a renowned spiritual teacher, said, "... everything that comes from love is a miracle." I did not give into fear and insecurities, but rather I remained open to the infinite possibilities life offers. I believe my dedication to living from a place of love created these experiences. Trust in the goodness of Life and the door will open for your miracles too.

When we quiet our minds, listen to the wise voice within, look for signs that direct us on our path and do what feels right, then we will see synchronicities and miracles happening. The important part is to be open to it; then even the smallest events can lead to miracles that change our lives. These moments of Grace remind us about the wonder and mystery of life.

I lovingly dedicate this chapter to an inspiring artist and free spirit Magda DaMag, my Soul Friend, teacher and guru. And, to all my caring and supportive friends. I am truly blessed to have you all in my life.

My heart is overflowing with gratitude as Life leads me from darkness… through wonder …to joy and miracles.

Many thanks to Izabela Jaroszynski, my lovely editor, for her assistance with this chapter.

A big thank you to Lisa Hardwick for her heartfelt inspiration, encouragement, and guidance. My life is blessed because of you. Thank you Lisa!

~ Halina Kurowska

Sharon Gambrill

SHARON GAMBRILL (also fondly known as 'Shazza') is a Sydney based comedian, actor, writer, Laughter Yoga Leader, and certified and licensed Heal Your Life® Workshop Teacher and Personal Coach. During a year of medical and holistic treatment following a mastectomy in 2011, Sharon decided it was time to 'go within' to examine the mind/body health connection and come to terms with a worried childhood being her mother's parent, her mother's subsequent suicide in 2001, absent father abandonment issues, and her lifelong struggle with obesity. It was a transformational time with healing occurring on a deep emotional level by studying the philosophies of Louise L. Hay and using her bestselling book, *You Can Heal Your Life* as a guide. Other healthy practices used were laughter, nutrition, Tapping, Reiki, walking, meditation, music, and visualization. Sharon always writes from the heart and is warm, open, honest, funny, and inspiring, Sharon continues to uplift everyone around her and is now on a personal mission to encourage others to accept themselves unconditionally, release the past, and create a miraculous life filled with love, laughter, and excellent health!

www.sharongambrill.com
info@sharongambrill.com
Or connect with her on Facebook, Twitter, Instagram or Meetup.

A Miraculous Move!

My mini Collins Gem Dictionary and Thesaurus from 1993 describes a Miracle as: "supernatural event, marvel" and Miraculous as: "amazing, extraordinary, incredible, marvellous, supernatural, unaccountable, wonderful, wondrous." I like the way those words sound! Doesn't it fill your mind with endless possibilities? Google describes a Miracle as:"an extraordinary and welcome event that is not explicable by natural or scientific laws and is therefore attributed to divine agency" plus "a remarkable event or development that brings welcome consequences" Sign me up for both of those!

We used to associate the word Miracle with crashing thunder and an old man with a long white beard appearing as the skies opened up to a dazzling light display, but in our modern world through the discoveries of physicists and neuroscientists we know that our brain emits a brain wave or frequency that can be measured and attracts similar thoughts and experiences back to us like a magnet. Such films as *You Can Heal Your Life, What The Bleep Do We Know,* and *The Secret,* feature a panel of experts who confirm this exciting scientific fact. This means we can begin right now to manifest our own miracles using the quantifiable power of our own brain using positive feelings and intentions. How exciting!

I had my own version of a Miracle at a time when I really needed one and was ready to make a move both literally and figuratively. Some years ago I was living in an old, damp, depressing apartment in an old, damp, depressing block of units. It was comfortable and affordable, but I was beginning to feel old, damp and depressed myself! I deserved a healthier and brighter place to live, but didn't want to spend more money, so I lived there for years. I felt really stuck. I justified that I was saving money for more important things such as overseas travel and buying my own home, but ultimately I just didn't think I deserved somewhere better. I went back and forth in my mind for years wanting to move out but blocking any way it could happen.

It wasn't until I was really ready to move somewhere better, and believed I deserved it, that it actually happened.

One Tuesday night I exclaimed out loud, "It's time, I'm ready to move. I deserve better. I really mean it now!" I made a definite decision and felt good about it. I didn't know how I would do it, I just decided it was time. Two nights later on the Thursday night at one of my regular places of work I was talking to someone and was prompted to ask how their week had been which was unusual as we usually only discussed work matters. They replied that they had just moved into a fabulous new home found through a website which I thought only specialised in buying and selling items. If that person hadn't been there we would never have had that conversation, but because I was ready to make the move I was guided in the right direction. When I got home that night, I checked the real estate section of that website and there listed only that afternoon was a lovely looking very private garden flat! I emailed the owners and we arranged a private viewing on the Saturday. I submitted the application form on the Monday and was approved on the Wednesday. All in under a week! Miraculous!

So many mini miracles were a part of this new home. I am allergic to grass, there was no grass anywhere on the property as it had all been removed to make way for concrete (I am not allergic to concrete!) and there were large garden beds of organic vegetables which I was told I could pick as many as I wanted. I had added more vegetables to my diet in recent years so that was a real bonus. The garden flat itself had previously been used as a converted beauty salon, so it had an extra wash basin in the bedroom and bathroom in the exact colour and design I like, plus the whole place smelt faintly of essential oils, so refreshing compared to the smell of mould in the old apartment! The surrounding streets were lined with lovely homes and happy families. I heard children laughing in their backyards and saw them playing at the local park with their fathers, something I had missed out on growing up, so I really enjoyed seeing these delightful families together. The apartment had been freshly painted, I had my own private washing line, a brand new kitchen and separate pantry which housed the fridge, something I had always wanted. Included was a garage, and a sea view in the distance towards my favourite local beach. The owners of the property who lived in a large farmhouse at the top of the property were respectful and kind, even bringing me home-made cookies as a welcome gift! I had air-conditioning and electricity was included so I was cool in Summer and warm in Winter. The flat had two separate entry doors and felt so large I thought I was living in a house. I had been affirming that I wanted to live in a house without any idea of how it would happen or how I could afford it, but nonetheless it felt like a house, so that demonstrates the power of an affirmation. Then there were the huge sunflowers that greeted me growing down the driveway leading to my flat. Next to the sunflowers stood a huge and beautiful flowering frangipani tree. My beloved Mother's favourite flowers were sunflowers and frangipanis, so I felt I had been given an extra blessing.

Despite the dire predictions of news reports and people telling me there was no affordable housing in Sydney, that the rental market was competitive with prospective tenants submitting extensive resumes and offering to pay more than the asking price in secret deals with real estate agents, I miraculously found a lovely and unique living situation easily which was completely affordable. I felt guided in the right direction at all times. When I had made up my mind, everything came together through the Law of Attraction, or the principles of quantum physics, or Divine Intelligence, however you perceive it. Everything lined up so my Miracle was invited into my life because I was ready to receive it. Perfect timing!

After moving in I walked around my new home appreciating each special part of it that was all ideal for me and thought it truly was a Miracle. This new place had come along when I needed it and when I was absolutely ready to make a change. I took action to bring it about and was willing to accept it. So let's do some calming exercises to get you in a relaxed and receptive state of mind so you can bring about, manifest, and receive your own Miracles!

1. Deep Breathing – Sit in a comfortable chair, put phones on silent, and minimise all noise. Close your eyes. Breathe in slowly through the nose to a count of four, hold for four, exhale through the mouth to a count of four. Do this three times.

2. Affirmations – Open your eyes, smile, and say these Louise L. Hay Power Thought Card Affirmations aloud. Be calm and don't think about how something will happen, or push for it, come to the understanding that it will happen at the perfect time and in the perfect way for you. *I Am Open And Receptive To All The Good And Abundance In The Universe - Divine Wisdom Guides Me - I Trust The Process Of Life - I Deserve The Best And I Accept The Best Now - I Open New Doors To Life - As I Say Yes To Life, Life Says Yes To Me - I Am A Magnet For Miracles* - Now take a deep breath in and exhale. Always say an affirmation in the positive, present tense as though it has already happened. Feel happy and enthusiastic as you say them, write them down, and look at them, as this reinforces the idea in your subconscious mind that you are deserving. This will also create new neural pathways in your brain which will send out such a powerful and energetic signal that you will begin to attract what you are seeking and give your Miracle a nudge in your direction! Even if it seems unrealistic keep going, and you will find the impossible seems possible.

3. Create a picture or vision board filled with pictures or photos, or just look at something by itself like a lovely home cut out of a real estate brochure. A visual of something really does reinforce in your subconscious mind that want you want is achievable, and that is when your mind and heart open up for Miracles to occur. I had taken photos of my favourite house 18 months earlier when I used to go for walks around the suburb I used to live in. It seemed impossible that I could afford such a house for myself. Then the same exact design of house (and I mean the same!) was magically the neighbouring house right behind my new garden apartment. I got to admire it every day when I got into my car and when I drove back down the driveway. I could look at it through my bedroom window. As I went out and came back every day I would marvel at this house and how beautiful it was. Another Miracle!

4. Laugh! Research shows laughter produces a response in the part of our brain that releases endorphins and other healthy hormones into our blood stream which improve our immune system and assist in cellular repair. Turn off the news and watch a funny movie or TV show. My Laughter Yoga workshops demonstrate that we can laugh doing fun laughter activities and pretend laughter to receive the same health benefits as if we are laughing for real. Pretend laughter in a group becomes real laughter very quickly anyway. Feeling lighthearted and free brings you a feeling of relief, and when you are feeling free you are more willing to accept the possibility of a Miracle in your life.

So whatever you are wishing for or thinking about, just know that it is possible. That when you let go of all fears and doubts and are truly ready, everything will line up for you to attract your Miracle. What's needed is an open mind to know it is possible, a feeling gratitude in anticipation, and the belief that you are deserving. Miracles comes in all shapes and sizes. They are available to us and can fall at your feet, or be gradually presented to you so that when you look back at the situation or event you realise that is was truly miraculous! I wish you a joyous experience attracting everything that helps you to feel peace, inner calm, happiness, love, and laughter because feeling like that is a Miracle in itself!

 "Miracles come in moments. Be ready and willing"

~ DR WAYNE DYER

I dedicate this chapter to anyone who needs a Miracle in their life. You are deserving, you are wonderful, you are uniquely you. You are already a Miracle so that's the first one down! The rest are available so open your mind and heart and trust they will come in at the perfect time for you. Mine did and so will yours!

I would like to acknowledge and thank Louise L. Hay and her ground breaking book, You Can Heal Your Life. This book literally changed my life! I would also like to acknowledge my beautiful and sensitive mother Lesley. My mother was the person who gave me a personally signed copy of You Can Heal Your Life after she met Louise in Sydney in 1986. A special mention goes to the wonderful and inspiring work of Oprah and Ellen DeGeneres who are role models of mine with their example of combining sincerity, positivity, and humour in their careers. Truly miraculous media workers!

~ Sharon Gambrill

Kelly Vass

KELLY VASS is her own Best Friend, Scott's Wife, Matt's Mother, Abby's Mother, and a licensed Heal Your Life ® Teacher and Life Coach.

She resides in Sherwood Park, Alberta, Canada, where she enjoys having fun with her family, reading, learning, writing, curling, cooking, nature walks, meaningful conversations, encouraging dreams, manifesting miracles, teaching workshops, coaching, all her Spiritual practices, and creating peace in the now.

Kelly is a student and teacher of love. Through her lived experiences of being a recovering perfectionist and a recovering people-pleaser, she has learned to create kind and loving boundaries for herself so that she can assist others in creating kind and loving boundaries in their lives. She assists people in remembering how truly amazing and brilliant they are.

inthenowkellyvass@shaw.ca
www.inthenowkellyvass.com
www.facebook.com/inthenowkellyvass/

Jessica,
Believe that you are deserving of all Miracles because you are!

Thank you for showing up as a Divine Miracle in my life!

In the now and always,
Kelly Vass

She Chose Happily Ever After

Once upon this lifetime, there was a little girl who loved miracles and she believed in them with all her heart. Her family called her Kelly Ann. "Ann is her middle name and there is no hyphen; she will be called Kelly Ann until such a time that she chooses otherwise" were the instructions. Like many little girls, Kelly Ann was told and believed that she could be and do anything she wanted to when she grew up. Around the age of five, people started taking an interest in what that might be.

Many asked "Kelly Ann, what do you want to be when you grow up?" Her reply, "I would like to be a Catholic priest." She received responses like: "you can't because you are a girl; you mean that you would like to be a Catholic nun; girls are not allowed to be priests." This confused Kelly Ann. She did not understand the human made rules of religion. At a Spirit level she desired to be a student and teacher of love. She knew that she was capable, so the word "can't" did not make sense to her. In her heart she knew that God and Jesus love unconditionally; she suspected that people create fear. She continued to answer "Catholic Priest" to the question. Each time that she did, her childlike enthusiasm and belief in self was replaced with a questioning of whether she was good enough for self, parents, relatives, school, her church, and perhaps her Spirit, Jesus, Mary, and God. She was sensitive and teased often. She was learning that perfection and pleasing others were rewarded at school and at home. She was a rule follower and she desired peace. In time, she changed her answer to "nun" so that those around her felt more comfortable. Her heart and Spirit screamed inside: "I desire to be a loving and kind priest when I grow up!" In junior high the teasing and bullying became too painful for Kelly Ann. Most people called her "Sister Kelly" and her belief in miracles was slipping away. Her answer to the question soon changed to "I don't know". Kelly loved caring for and playing with children. In the presence of children, Kelly Ann was happy and she felt safe to be herself. Kelly thought if she could not be a Catholic priest, maybe it was time to choose a new dream: "I don't know what I want to do when I grow up, but I know that my biggest dream is to be a Mother."

By the time Kelly was in secondary school, there were so many more activities, people, and requests that she felt required a yes; perfection became her expectation for every area of her life. Kelly never felt that she ever had permission to say no in her life and this had painful consequences. Life felt like a struggle all the time. The overwhelm, worry, stress, and anxiety resulted in crying herself to sleep many nights. She was exhausted all the time and her health suffered. In high school she was diagnosed with Chronic Fatigue Syndrome. Even when life is being experienced as a struggle and one is ready to throw in the towel, Spirit finds a way of miraculously sending an absolute yes, that serves their highest good. Scott arrived as a shy boy who timidly asked Kelly for a Christmas card at the curling rink when they were fifteen. He soon became Kelly's best friend. He was the fun and funny guy who did not take things or himself too seriously, enjoyed to laugh, under committed in order to go with the flow of life, and radiated a deep and respectful kindness with a quick wit. Their friendship became her safe place. Kelly moved out on her own at age nineteen, stopped going to college, worked two jobs including working for her parents' business, and continued to please everyone. She created a pattern of doing things for herself when, and if, all the work and pleasing others was completed. This might happen somewhere between 9:00 P.M. and 4:00 A.M. The value of sleep was not valued or learned in her family of origin. The person who made certain that there was some fun in Kelly's life was Scott. After ten years of friendship, Scott kissed Kelly and they started dating; less than two years later, Kelly proposed to him and received a suspenseful, yet quick yes.

Kelly became hopeful. Kelly and Scott really enjoyed planning their wedding celebration and the day was perfect. The first year of marriage was a dream come true and Kelly started feeling a bit of the peace that she yearned for. She was starting to believe in miracles again.

They started visualizing their next greatest dream: Kelly and Scott would like to be parents. They both agreed that they would be relaxed about conceiving. They both had amazing work ethics that translated into long hours and some pressures, so it was important to decrease stress in their home. This lasted for a bit. Kelly was very good at her work but she did not enjoy it. It actually drained and depleted her in almost every way but she did not know how to leave. She still had not learned to say no to that which did not work for her. Part of Kelly's biggest dream coming true would include her leaving work to be an at home Mother.

Most of Kelly's friends were having children. She was impatient for her biggest dream to start now! Kelly knew her cycle so well and she was starting to get scared.

It had been a couple years of trying and the miracle of life was really starting to feel like it might be out of reach. This terrified her. Throughout her life, Kelly's answer to any struggle was to work harder. Kelly formed the idea that if she could be the perfect wife, perfect daughter, perfect sister, perfect employee, perfect home-maker, perfect friend, perfect Catholic, perfect student, perfect hostess, and perfect person, God might grant her a miracle. Unfortunately, she projected this idea onto her husband without communicating that she was shifting away from the relaxed, "letting it happen."

Kelly and Scott were gifted with a new question at the beginning of their marriage: "when are you having children?" At first they answered "in a couple of years" or "when it happens". The question was becoming more and more painful to answer. Every month was a roller coaster of emotion of high and hopeful anticipation to very low and sad disappointment. For Scott, he just wanted to be happy. If it was with kids, great, if it wasn't, everything would be okay. For Kelly it had become a need. She thought that conceiving would be proof that she was good enough, worthy, and lovable. She saw fertility as the road to happiness and the elusive feeling of joy. Kelly was getting more exhausted at work. At home, Kelly and Scott were constantly saying yes to birthday parties and events for miraculous, fun, and loving children. It was a constant reminder of what was missing.

Kelly needed a new focus and it arrived from every direction. At work, the position that she was working towards had been awarded to someone more qualified. Kelly's biggest cheer-leader, Grandma Frances, took her last breath after a longer than expected stay in palliative care. Kelly received the exciting news that her sister was expecting her first child. Kelly was burned-out at work and at home and she needed change. She decided to resign from her job of eleven years and go back to school. She took a year to upgrade her sciences and she was accepted as a nursing student. Her perfectionism and pleasing achieved a new level. The change allowed Kelly to open up a bit more spiritually and some of her mentors became the authors' words in the books that she was reading. She was doing well in school and she was enjoying learning and she also had some deep emotional wounds and feelings of not being good enough that were being measured constantly by fear, marks, and self-evaluation. Kelly's inner critic was louder than ever. Kelly created another idea in her head: If she started her nursing education, she would probably get pregnant within the first year. That did not happen and the pain, sadness, and loneliness of her experience of infertility increased every month. As a nursing student she had unlimited access to fertility research papers. At the beginning of the second year of nursing school, Kelly and Scott decided to take the next step and visit a fertility specialist. After every diagnostic that could be completed without causing harm, a diagnosis of unexplained infertility was given, including very low statistical chances of conceiving without medical intervention. Now, the medical interventions are quite invasive to the natural female hormone balance and there is high risk of multiples including the possibility of creating situations where major ethical decisions are required. Scott and Kelly decided that Kelly would finish her nursing degree and then they would revisit this. They had a new answer to the question, "unexplained infertility."

It turned out that everyone who heard the words "unexplained infertility" wanted an explanation. Kelly and Scott were not prepared for the reactions and questions. Kelly being very low on assertiveness felt the need to explain. Now, with fertility, there is one test for the male and if he passes, they move on to explore the female. There are a couple more tests for the female and then after that it is a mystery. Scott passed his test. What everyone seemed to want to know was where the problem was? Kelly felt defective and that it was all her fault. Scott would lovingly say that "fertility is a 'we' problem and we are in this together."

Kelly put everything she had into school and she finished her 3rd year of nursing with a perfect GPA and strangely, the lowest self-esteem and assertiveness of her life. Her life was school, caring for the house, and saying yes to everyone else. Her self-doubt replaced intuition and her inner critic was strong and mean. Anxiety was controlling her life. It was really difficult for her to hear any whispers of her heart.

Then a series of events took place that transformed her life.

First, Kelly sought treatment for anxiety; she was learning self-hypnosis to return her worrying mind to the present moment and find her calm. Self-hypnosis assisted Kelly with hearing the whispers of her heart and breathing. Prior to this, others' voices were loudest.

Second, Kelly practiced her art of hiding in plain view at a good friend's baby shower. Kelly completely embraced the role of victim. She thought that she was ready for the question: "when are you and your husband planning to have a family?" Kelly replied "we have experienced over 7 years of unexplained infertility." A person sitting across from Kelly interjected with compassion: "I am so sorry for your loss. Have you mourned and grieved for your infertility?" Tears came to Kelly's eyes and no one including Kelly knew what to say. This lovely earth angel continued: "it is a deep loss every month; have you mourned?" Kelly answered "no, I don't think that I have." It was a profound day voicing the shared and lived experience of unexplained infertility with another. Kelly returned home that evening and began her journey of grieving her infertility and in doing so, somehow accepting where she was at.

Third, a trusted friend recommended that Kelly read *The Power of Now: A Guide to Spiritual Enlightenment* written by Eckhart Tolle. After doing so she said to her friend: "it is a lovely concept and I desire being in the now but I think that I need the power of how." Her friend's response was "then you may want to begin with *You Can Heal Your Life* by Louise Hay." Kelly replied "Hey, I have that book. It practically jumped off the shelf at the bookstore recently so I bought it. I have not read it yet. Thank you." *You Can Heal Your Life* was Spirit sent to Kelly during one of the darkest times in her life. This book was a miracle as it created a willingness to love herself again. It was indeed the answer to all her how questions as it had effective tools and exercises. She started going to bed nightly, listening to vocal affirmations that accompany Louise's book *I Can Do It*. As Kelly prioritized loving herself in the now, her inner strength, power, and love were returning. This was a slow process but she was not measuring. There was a strong desire for peace; she started really liking herself again and her belief in miracles slowly returned.

That fall, classes resumed. Kelly sat down with her coffee next to a friend in class and she mentioned how awful it tasted. Her friend said that hers was great and she asked if she could taste Kelly's. Her friend told her that it tasted fine and she asked if Kelly could possibly be pregnant. Her friend said that when she was pregnant, coffee tasted funny. It was so painful to even think about taking another pregnancy test. Breathe Kelly. That evening she took the over-the-counter test and she asked Scott to retrieve it. The look on his face was similar to the look he had when he said yes to Kelly's marriage proposal. She started shaking when she looked at it and she softly said "it has never looked like this before." She called her doctor and he congratulated her. This surprised her. He told her that the home tests are extremely accurate. In that moment she knew. She knew that miracles exist and she knew that they are manifested by love for self. She vowed in that moment that she would learn to love herself as much as Kelly could love so that she could love her miracles as much as Mommy could love!

There is gratitude that comes out of the struggle and it allows me to see all the miracles of my story. Every single day I quote Laura Krauss Melmed to Kelly Ann and my children: "I love you as much as a mother can love." Our happily ever after is described on a plaque that Scott gifted me. It hangs on the wall between the bedrooms of our two miracles.

Once in a while right in the middle of an ordinary life love gives us a Fairy Tale.

~ UNKNOWN

Dedicated to the brave and courageous and powerful that are willing to love themselves!

I am filled with grace and gratitude for all the teachers who have appeared and continue to appear when this student is ready! "When the student is ready, the teacher appears" (Hay, 1991, p.75). Thank you Jody Gotell for reintroducing me to my Spirit! Thank you Jessica Tyson Salkeld for communicating the ways I may serve in love! Thank you Kami Anderson Moreno for stating "you are a writer." Thank you Brenda Fedorchuk and Lisa Hardwick for your patience, kindness, and love! Thank you Darrel and Dorothy Sutton, family, and friends for being my first teachers and for cheering me on!

~Kelly Vass

Amy Pazahanick

AMY PAZAHANICK is a professional athlete, author, motivational speaker and successful entrepreneur. As the Founder and CEO of Agape Ventures, Amy has built her business and life around the core principle of unconditional love or "agape." She is dedicated to empowering others to create their own authentic "playbooks" for achieving peak potential.

Amy lives in Roswell, Georgia where she operates Agape Tennis Academy. Her articles on mental self-mastery, and sports and business performance have been featured in the *Huffington Post* and dozens of other magazines across the nation.

When she's not coaching on the courts or captivating audiences with her "game changing" success strategies, Amy enjoys cuddling up with her two cats to read, playing golf, listening to Frank Sinatra music, and traveling to exotic corners of the world to experience new cultures and cuisine.

amy@agape-ventures.com
www.agape-ventures.com

The Birthday Miracle

It is July twenty-first, 2006 and I am sitting in a psychologist's office. It would be unusually hard to remember this date except for the fact this happens to be my twenty-first birthday. In front of me is a middle-aged, overweight, balding man by the name of Dr. Mathis. The office is bleak, with shades of beige and several book cases. I scan the books and see words like Gestalt Therapy, Sigmund Freud, and Operant Conditioning. I have no clue on what type of journey I am about to embark.

Why can't I be like every other college kid on their twenty-first birthday deciding what type of alcoholic beverage I want to be my first legal sip?

Instead, I am stuck talking to an unattractive middle-aged, man who is asking me absurd questions! When I am finally released from his interrogation, my parents greet me in the parking lot and ask me what I want to have for my birthday dinner. Finally, a question that I am happy to answer. I am so relieved to be heading home to have a celebratory dinner with my family, even though I know something is desperately off course with my life.

No Man's Land

But let's back up, and let me tell you how I got here. Three days before my twenty-first birthday, I travelled home from the University of Florida where I had been competing in a tennis tournament. Playing tennis has always been one of my talents. In fact, I played extensively in competitions as early as age eight and it has been one of the most important things in my life. Because of this sport, I was fortunate enough to earn a tennis scholarship to Coastal Carolina University where I soaked up the sun and went surfing every chance I got. It was also during this time that I started getting stoned and binge drinking more than I'd like to admit.

I was literally on a "high" from my performance at my latest competition when I walked through the door of my childhood home. But the "buzz" of my big win came crashing down when I saw the look on my parents' faces. "Amy we need to talk.

What are these things I've found in your closet? What do you think you are doing? Are you crazy?? Are you trying to ruin your life?"

They had found all of my pot paraphernalia, which at the time, was quite extensive. My room was practically a smoke shop, with an array of bowls and bongs mixed in with my tennis balls and shoes. My parents were in shock... and off to Dr. Mathis's I went.

There's Got to Be Something More

Fast forward four months, and it's now November 2006. I'm more open to Dr. Mathis and I am even starting to enjoy talking to him, but I have no idea how this is going to make a difference in my life. I am trying my best not to smoke pot and make poor choices but nothing seems to be working. Internally, I am beating myself down with negative self-talk that makes me feel worthless. There is an inner pain I cannot escape. I am so unhappy. I cannot name this pain or where it came from. I am trying so hard to change.

Why is nothing getting better for me?

My mind is questioning everything and my lack of answers fills me with anxiety and fear. Why can't I get off this train? Why do I keep making the same stupid choices when I genuinely want to change? Why is this so hard?

Why am I even alive? Maybe I should just kill myself... what is the point anyway? These were the thoughts that were haunting my mind as feelings of hopelessness overcame me. All I wanted to do was to escape. Tears ran down my face as I sank deeper into the darkness.

For the first time in my life, I prayed out loud, "*God, Goddess, Higher Power, whatever you are, show me you exist and that there is more to this world than what I can see, please help me?*

I need to know <u>NOW</u> that you exist.

I cannot go on without this knowledge. I cannot do this by myself. Help me." Soon my salty tears begin to subside and a gentle calm comes over me. A sense of peace and relaxation replaces my dread and something pulls me from my bed where I am weeping. I walk towards my desk. There I see the book that my mother has given me two Christmases ago. It is Marianne Williamson's book *A Gift of Change* and the title seems to be speaking directly to me. I feverishly flip it open and find these words:

> Whenever we feel lost, or insane, or afraid, all we have to do is ask for His help. The help might not come in the form we expected, or even the thought we desired, but it will come, and we will recognize it by how we feel. In spite of everything, we will feel at peace.
>
> ~ MARIANNE WILLIAMSON

Were these words written just for me? I've been wanting to change. I re-read the title and hungrily scan the entire book in astonishment. With each word I read, I feel tears of joy- not sadness welling up inside me now. I cannot believe this is happening. If this is not God talking directly to me, then I do not know who it is! I flip to the front of the book and find these words on the first page:

> Behold, I tell you a mystery: We shall not all sleep, but we shall all be changed-in a moment, in the twinkling of an eye, at the last trumpet. For the trumpet will sound, and the dead will be raised incorruptible, and we shall be changed.
>
> ~ CORINTHIANS 15:51-52

It is 2:30 am in the morning and I can't put the book down. I have been reading through the night. I do not know what has just happened, but I know it is something powerful. Things have shifted. I can feel it. I have been heard.

On the Road to Find Out

From this day forward, I begin the process of knowing this higher power and allowing it to guide my life. I begin devouring hundreds of spiritual, self-help, and psychology books to understand the source of my suffering. Marianne Williamson and Wayne Dyer become my metaphysical and spiritual mother and father. I read every book each of them has ever written. Every word helps me to understand, and most importantly accept who I am! I acknowledge that I am a composite of my upbringing, my opinions and beliefs. I question and analyze EVERYTHING! I take particular interest in learning about my parent's and grandparent's heritage to better understand myself. I psychoanalyze every aspect of my being. I become deeply interested in meditation, prayer, and yoga and exploring anything that can help me reconnect and *stay connected* with the beautiful, loving Source I felt that fateful evening.

My interest in psychology classes soars and I begin watching movies that chronicle the life experiences of athletes whose lives are similar to mine. In particular, I am impacted by the movie *The Peaceful Warrior* that illustrates how an athlete is able to overcome his ego and transcend it through similar mind-body practices. I see myself in this athlete. I write my final essay for my Sports Psychology class on the movie and receive a perfect score. My tennis game and grades improve. I gradually and then eventually stop smoking altogether. I am seeing my life altered before my eyes. *I have given myself the gift of change.*

I am different, and the world even looks different to me. It seems more vivid and fragrant. The sun is brighter, the seasons crisper and the leaves on the trees are more colorful. Who knew? I am on a natural high! *A miracle has occurred.*

I thank God. More than a decade later, I pray and meditate daily. I ask Source to help me use all of my gifts and to never waste any of them again. I have found the key to unlocking my potential and it is through staying connected to that all-knowing Source.

Staying Powered Up

There is a power much greater than us in this world. As I journey through life, I vow never to forget this miraculous moment or take it for granted. Like any good relationship, I have to nurture it. I have to take the time to stay connected with this eternal "power" Source, so I am able to use all of my potential while I am on Earth.

Sometimes I find maintaining my connection, even after having such a strong and life-altering event can be challenging, especially when my schedule feels overwhelming. Here are some simple ways you can keep God/Source first and foremost in your life to tap into all of your potential, even when life is moving fast.

Take time to meditate first thing in the morning. Set aside an extra fifteen minutes to meditate each morning. Sit completely still, clear your mind and get silent so you can hear Source. Try closing your eyes and repeating a mantra for the day, or simply try to empty your mind. What is it trying to tell you? Maybe even keep a journal close by so you can write down the thoughts that come to you after you finish your meditation. It is amazing how much more in tune you will be with synchronicities when you intentionally align with spirit each day.

Listen to positive or inspirational music or audio messages on your way to work, lunch, meetings or other destinations. This will put you in a positive state of mind without requiring much on your part. Immerse yourself in positive, uplifting music and messages as you drive. It can alter your state of mind and remind you of your connection to all of life and Source. It can help you hit the spiritual "reset" button and remind you to be your absolute best.

Keep inspirational quotes around your house or workplace. I strategically place quotes all around my home to continuously stay inspired and live my life to its greatest potential.

Use positive affirmations and visualize your success. Talk positively out loud to yourself as a tool to program your mind to think positively. ***Speak the things you want to appear in your life into existence.*** Visualize yourself with your dream job, spouse, home, or car. You can use a vision board and literally post pictures of the things you wish to attract. Be sure to place these images in a location where you can frequently focus on them. As a general rule, the first thing in the morning and before bedtime is the best time to visualize. While you sleep, the universe will be working hard to bring you what you have visualized.

Give up the power to get the power. Remember, there is a power greater than you that you can tap into at any time. Source is always guiding you. You are never alone. Sometimes we wish for things that are not really in our highest and greatest good, so remember if something does not work out the way you would have wished, more than likely something more magnificent is on its way. Source is working 24/7, 365 days a year behind the scenes on your behalf!

You will feel fully alive and on fire with life when you are using your gifts to their highest and greatest capacity. There are times when you may feel like you are in a rut and self-doubt may threaten to drag you down. Taking the time to reconnect or connect for the first time to a power greater than yourself, whether through meditation, prayer, yoga, or another form, can help you remember who you really are and what you have been placed on this planet to do. When you get back in alignment with your purpose, you can never feel anything less than miraculous.

Dedicated to my mother and father, Betsy and Andy Pazahanick

I am deeply grateful: To Jennifer Wadsworth, my friend, neighbor, editor, constant encourager, and soul sister. To David Benzel, my friend and mentor, for always being in my corner. To Cari Covahey and Trish Hanson, your friendships and unwavering support mean the world to me. To everyone who is or has ever been a part of Agape Tennis Academy; especially my sweet students who fill me with so much joy. To my mother and father for everything they are. To each of you, your support means everything. Agape.

-Amy Pazahanick

Dr. Scott Ferreira

DR. SCOTT FERREIRA is a licensed Chiropractic Physician, a fellow in Acupuncture, a workshop leader, an Ordained Minister and certified life and wellness coach serving the Seacoast of New England for the past 17 years. His passion is to help individuals achieve optimal health within the Wellness model and help guide them to living the life that they desire most.

He is the co-owner of Natural Care Wellness Center with his wife Dr. Jody Ferreira in Eliot Maine. They have four amazing children and travel the country challenging themselves in running, biking and obstacle races.

Together they use a "whole person" wellness approach to healing in order to help accelerate and/or maintain your journey to great health. This approach to wellness means looking for underlying causes of physical, emotional, nutritional, chemical, environmental, and spiritual disturbances and disruptions leading to illness and dis-ease.

Drscott99@gmail.com
www.naturalcarewellness.com

A Divine Journey of the Heart

It was a beautiful New England day in mid-September. I had just finished seeing patients at my Wellness clinic. There is a gentle calm that settles in the practice as the day winds down and the day's healings that unfolded still linger in the air. I walked into my office and glanced out the window to observe the sky morphing into evening with exquisite autumn colors. The leaves were falling with a gentle breeze causing the radiant colors of apricot, coral, and mustard to swirl before me. Transfixed by the beauty, I was profoundly grateful for the interconnectivity of each of our lives with the natural world and with the one who created it all, GOD. I was reminded of how these connections allow our hearts to remain open, and in doing so, allows Divine guidance to be received.

The natural transformations of Earth through the seasons are reflected in our own lives as we grow and change. When our internal vibration, created by the atoms in our cells, matches the vibration of our surroundings, a synchronicity is created. When two or more atoms become synchronic, they create a vibrational harmony. When one is attuned to this vibration, we become more aware of our environment and begin to open our hearts. If we are able to perceive this, we are open to receiving messages from the Divine. Nature has a great way of opening this pathway so that we can be in receivership of messages from GOD, leading to everyday miracles. Our egos will more times than not block this pathway. I was once at a conference listening to the late Dr. Wayne Dyer when he explained that "the longest journey a person will ever take is 18 inches; that is the distance from their head to their heart." This statement has affected me profoundly and I use it every day to remove the blockades of my own ego's control to allow miracles to manifest.

As I stood at the window, I felt a deep peace within my heart. I thanked the Creator of the Universe for all this splendor and for allowing me to experience the

Divine presence of life. One of my office staff called out a goodnight as she left out the back door, which brought me back to the moment and to the physical world. I said goodnight and proceeded to grab my jacket and keys to leave the clinic. This evening was to be the first night of practice for a community choir where I had been singing for eight years. We were returning from our summer hiatus, and were to begin preparations for the winter performance. As I left the office, a deep voice said, **"You are not going to practice tonight!"** I was stopped in my tracks. There was no one in the room with me. The building I was in was empty. I sat in a chair and just took a minute to collect my thoughts. Nothing like this had happened to me before. I sat and meditated asking for clarity on what I had just heard. In the past, I have always been very intuitive, but I usually received messages by feelings or ideas, never by a voice. One of the things I had been working on recently was discernment of intuitive wisdom from the Divine. I wanted to trust that what I was receiving was coming from GOD and not my own ego.

Over the past two years, I had developed a system of discernment that provided me guidance. If I received intuitive information, I would wait for that message to be confirmed through three separate encounters at three distinct times before taking action. This system has helped me to trust that the intuitive information that I receive is from a Divine source and not my own ego. On occasion it would take weeks to months to receive three confirmations of the message; other times, just days. Up until this day, it had never taken place in a matter of minutes or hours.

I finished mediating, and got up and left the office. As I was walking to the car, I once again looked around the parking lot and took in all the beauty nature had to offer. It was dusk and the sky was vibrant with the hues of violet, salmon, rose, and amber. I sat in my car for a few minutes and decided that I would head to choir anyway, particularly since I only heard the message once. As I was driving to practice I heard again, **"You are not going to practice tonight!"** I immediately pulled the car over and stopped on the side of the road. I could not ignore the message, but I was confused. "Why…?" I started to ask, but received no reply. Sometimes in life we are not given the "whys," but we have to trust what we receive. I decided to change my plans and head home. As I drove, I had this overwhelming feeling to drive over to a sacred walking labyrinth that in the past has brought me clarity.

Labyrinths can be great tools for discernment and for connecting closer to the Divine. Ancient cultures appear to have taken care to place these sacred paths over specific areas of the Earth with favorable vibrations by using dowsing tools and geomancers in order to locate the energy vortex. They are designed to be prayer and meditative paths to help you along your journey in life to receive wisdom, discernment, health, and miracles. One of the most famous labyrinths in the world is in

Chartres Cathedral outside of Paris, France. This sacred site was built in 1200AD and acted as a pilgrimage for early Christians to connect closer to GOD. They would use this 11 circuit labyrinth along with the Lord's Prayer to create miracles in their life. The labyrinth that I use is 7 circuit and is a captivating forest labyrinth hidden behind a local church.

As I stepped out of my car, I felt the crisp autumn air. The trees that line this forest were painted with gold, crimson, and peach. The entrance to the labyrinth was glowing with the Divine light of the setting sun. Everything just seemed to radiate as I entered the forest to the beginning of the labyrinth. I felt myself starting to sense and match the vibration of this space. This Labyrinth has a dirt floor and is marked by local rocks and stones that were dowsed and placed purposefully to locate an energy grid. I had learned in a spiritual workshop that one should pose a question, situation, or problem when entering a labyrinth, and ask for guidance or clarification and enlightenment.

I paused and started my journey into the labyrinth by saying a prayer asking for guidance about this choir concern. One of the things I enjoy doing occasionally, while walking in this space, is to sing. This seems to help me connect in with nature by raising my vibration, and to get out of my head and into my heart. I am then able to listen to the wisdom my soul has for me. As I began to walk and sing, I connected to the environment allowing nature to enrich my experience. I felt the sensation of the season, and some amusement that I was singing on this journey to seek answers about a choir issue.

In New England during September we experience "fall", which is a time nature transforms itself to prepare for the next season. Nature sheds what it does not need so that it can prepare to bloom anew; stronger, mightier, and greater. I recognized that I needed to shed my fears and the parts of my ego that block me from receiving Divine wisdom. I chose that day to drop those feelings like the leaves and allow the Divine into my heart. As I entered the center of the labyrinth called "the womb", I centered myself in my heart and asked for guidance. I said a deep heartfelt prayer and waited for an answer. One of the enchanting things built into a 7 circuit labyrinth is its connection to the Lord's Prayer. There are seven lessons to the Lord's Prayer that Kathleen McGowen writes in her book called *The Book of Love*. These seven lessons relate to the seven parts of the sacred labyrinth. The lessons are Faith, Surrender, Service, Abundance, Forgiveness, Overcoming Obstacles, and Love. As you walk the circuits, you reflect on each area as you pass through a circuit until you come to "the womb," which is love.

As I waited for my answer, a feeling of love overcame me. GOD gave me my next right step. I heard, **"Go down the street to the church on the hill tonight.**

There you will sing. They need you and you need them!" This surprised me. I knew of this church. I had taken a few classes at that location over the years but did not attend church there. At that time, my family attended another local church. As I left "the womb", I walked out of the labyrinth with my directive. I knew my next step. I thanked GOD and my soul for this guidance. As I drove down the street to the church on the hill, my ego started to go haywire. Fear and doubt set in and I began questioning my recent experience. My mind started to argue with me, insisting that I was making it all up. I felt that I could not just walk in there without knowing anything about their choir, if they had one, and if they were looking for singers. I truly felt confused and totally in the dark. This is common when your ego wants to regain control and block Divine direction. I centered myself, pushed through this fear and doubt, and decided to drive to the church anyway. At this point, it was around 6:25 on a Tuesday evening. I parked my car and nervously walked to the front door. My heart was pounding with anticipation. I opened the door of the church and the first person I saw was my teacher, Ellen, who I had taken a class from nine months earlier. She was surprised to see me and greeted me with a hug. Ellen asked what she could do for me. I inquired if they had a choir and if they were looking for any singers. To my amazement, she laughed and stated the choir was looking for people and they in fact had a practice that very night starting in a few minutes. From then, I was invited to stay and observe if I chose. I was amazed by this whole synchronistic event. Never in my life had I received direct Divine guidance so clearly and for a whole experience to unfold in such a short amount of time. What I later found out is that Ellen laughed because situations like mine happen all the time at this church. They are a spirit-led church that listen to the will of GOD for their guidance and direction.

At this point in my life, I began recognizing that miracles do happen every day. The synchronicity of life is there for us to see and be part of, if we choose. Sometimes in life, we become so caught up in the mundane minutia of living day-to-day, that we are not able to get to see or experience the miracles happening around or within us. That night, I decided to join the choir which inspired a whole new divine adventure in my life. I have met many great friends and a community of heart-centered souls. They have encouraged me and demonstrated to me evidence of miracles happening every day. Through more miracles, inspiration, and synchronicity, I found myself on the praise and worship team. My singing has greatly improved and my spiritual nature continues to grow more and more heart centered. My intuitive gifts have expanded to my singing and sharing the Spirit with others. Today, I find myself singing every week in front of hundreds of people with the intention of helping them all connect to their hearts.

As a Wellness Doctor, I am trained to diagnose and treat physical ailments. I coach and support patients to facilitate healing in a physical manner. The role that GOD has given me at this church is one I do not feel I would have chosen for myself or had the ability to accomplish. I was placed at that church on the hill for many reasons that are still unfolding every day. I believe GOD has a plan for each of us if we allow it to unfold. It is usually greater than anything we could have imagined and there are always great lessons and growth along the journey. It's a path filled with love, freedom, joy, and miracles. I feel blessed that I am able to connect with more people in different ways with every experience that is presented to me. In this church, I have been placed in a position to create a sacred space of healing and love through music. As one of the worship team members, we facilitate an environment of love and grace much like the center of the Labyrinths' womb. This allows individuals to feel safe to open their hearts to receive guidance, healing, and wisdom from the Divine. It is an honor and a privilege that GOD has given to me and I am deeply grateful for it. One of the profound lessons in life we all have to learn is that fear holds us back. Fear is an acronym for "false evidence appearing real", something I learned from a lecture by Louise Hay years ago. When we push through it, then miracles are allowed to happen to each and every one of us. The more miracles we experience, the more synchronistic we become with one another. We can all help each other create miracles, but we must first step up and take a chance and listen to the messages of our hearts. If we follow through with what we our heart guides us do, we make room for miracles to happen in our lives and for miracles to happen in others' lives.

I challenge you each day to take that 18-inch journey and connect to your heart. Listen to the love that exists there. Your soul and divine image are waiting for you there. Bravely push through the fears and anxiety that can set in. Your ego will block your divine potential if you allow it. Gratitude for life promotes happiness. Instead, trust that your potential is a life filled with miracles, and one of passion, love, and joy. Allow these traits to emanate for all to see. You create change in the world by first starting within. As the Universal spiritual law states, "as above, so below; as within, so without." Allow the Divine to help you see the beauty of life and the beauty that is within you. You are a spiritual being having a physical experience to create a life filled with miracles. In Gratitude and Infinite Blessings!

I dedicate this chapter to GOD for gracing me with a beautiful life and for the gift of healing to aid humanity. Secondly to my loving and supportive wife, Jody, and my four children, Jared, Evan, Logan, and Ella; I am blessed beyond measure to share this journey with you.

A special thank you to my Mom, Dad, and Sister for always believing in me and supporting my adventures. To my friends Marcia and Gano Adair, for your unconditional support and heartfelt laughter. To my friend Donna Tobey for your life encouragements, especially in writing. To my spiritual mentor Kelle Eli, for your deep wisdom towards Tree Of Life principals. To Suzanne Richardson, my friend and editor, just a heartfelt THANK YOU. Lastly to my church family at CLC and my work family at NCWC, I love you all and you help me grow as an individual every day.

-Scott Ferreira

Donna Jutras Tobey

DONNA JUTRAS TOBEY is passionate about living limitless possibilities out loud while teaching others how to do the same! She is a personal coach, mentor, workshop teacher, writer, and speaker. She is trained, certified, and licensed as a 'Heal Your Life' Workshop Teacher and Coach, based on the philosophies of Louise L. Hay.

Donna lives in New Hampshire with her son, Ian and two lively Maine coon cats, Arty and Ditey. All three boys keep her laughing! She is founder of You've Got Power Baby, inspiring everyone to find their answers WITHIN. Learn more at ygpowerbaby.com.

Mostly, she is a student of Life who allows Divine Intelligence to be her teacher!

www.ygpowerbaby.com

All I Need Is A Miracle

It was February in one of the snowiest winters on record. The snow just kept falling, creating an isolating igloo of icy cold. There wasn't much that was moving--especially in the housing market. There were few listings of homes for sale online, and even fewer open houses. But I began the search for my new home. I knew it was out there; we only had to find each other.

My son was graduating high school the beginning of June and my rental lease was up at the end of June. It was clear that I had to move. So it was time for me to set my intentions and think about what I wanted. At the minimum, I desired a property with a mother-in-law apartment or attached unit that I could rent out, to help with the mortgage and as an investment. This was my third move in four years, and I longed for a place to own and call my own. I was excited for this new adventure that awaited me!

Each morning upon waking, I would ask the Universe, "Where's my new home?" "Please show me my new home." I checked online sites, and put feelers out to friends and family in case they knew of any homes for sale. I contacted a friend's daughter who is a Realtor and contracted with her to start the process. I drove by listings and attended the few open houses--in snowstorms! --just to get a feeling for what was available in my price range. What I found was very dreary indeed, and the field was even more limited because I wanted the option of something I could rent out. This was all new to me, especially doing it as a newly single woman, alone.

At least, that's what my mind was telling me: that I'm alone. The truth is, I am never alone. I know that life is for me! Even when I needed to change rentals unexpectedly the year before, the perfect solution showed up with Divine timing. There is a flow to life that is positive and life-affirming, co-created from a place of heartfelt love and trust that the right answers always arrive.

When you make a decision to work with the Universe and allow *it* to teach you and show you the way, miracles happen! All I needed was a miracle.

The real-estate process continued to move forward slowly with few doors opening along the way. Thankfully, some of the financial pieces fell into place easily; that kept the positive flow of expectation and excitement alive.

Sifting and sorting through listing after listing, I saw many homes that were in my price range, but there was no option for a rental. And then, when I least expected it, it happened, in the place that I least expected. A town that I had lived in when I was in my twenties, with ancestral roots on my father's side. Growing up, I had many fond family memories with my grandparents, aunts, uncles and cousins. Then I remembered that as a young child, when my mom was still alive, we had lived there too.

But I was adamant: I was not living in this town, despite my Realtor asking me to just take a look at two properties. Finally, I agreed to look, still insisting that "I am *not* living in this town." Been there, done that! I had already lived there and was looking for something new, something with more "life," to suit my *new* life, moving forward.

Still, when you allow the Universe to guide you and you surrender to a living force that knows more than you do in your limited human capacity, unexpected possibilities show themselves. In short, miracles.

Before this, every house I'd looked at needed some major renovation. Until I walked into one of the houses in the town where I refused to live. It was the first place where my heart said, "I could live here." Plus, I could live here without having to renovate a thing! The price was even significantly less than I was willing to pay. To top it off, there were many, many extras I had not put on my wish list: including an in-ground swimming pool. This was something that I'd dreamed about for years and years! This home was well cared for, well loved, and just felt "right."

But…I did not want to live in that town.

As I was leaving the property after the first showing, I happened to glance at the listing agent's for-sale sign and noticed that she had the exact same married last name as my father's youngest sister. Many times when I was with my aunt, she'd notice her last name and say, "But this isn't spelled right." It was just something we shared. Well, *this* last name *was* spelled right! I smiled at the memory.

Truly, I was in that "stuck" place, not knowing what to do. My head and my heart were not in alignment. I was very resistant to "going backwards." Then the Universe whispered, "What if you are simply going home?" Listening to my heart, I remembered joyful memories with family and friends from years gone by. Several friends still lived in this same town and the thought of reconnection delighted me. The potential for new life did exist in this town, a mill town in the process of rebuilding. Before too long, I began to open my heart--and fall in love.

Whether I understood it or not, this property was calling to my heart. Connections continued to show up in unexpected ways, signs leading me along the way. Another ancestral connection was revealed when my father's other sister's last name, a *very* unusual last name, was the last name of my contact with the title company. Ancestors were making themselves known to me! I really felt that I was being called there.

My father only had two sisters. My father's oldest sister passed in her fifties. Within six months of her passing, my father's youngest sister's husband also passed. In time, the two remaining, married. Yes, my father's youngest sister married her older sister's husband! My aunt and uncle were very special to me. Our heart connection was undeniable. They married on my 25th birthday. Now the closing date for this property was scheduled on my birthday, their anniversary.

Like dominoes toppling one after the other, more connections started showing up. One night, my son came home from work very excited: he'd learned something interesting about our new home-to-be. This was a surprise. I'd cautioned him not to mention anything to anyone until we knew it was really happening. But when he'd signed into work that night, his supervisor questioned him about moving to New Hampshire. Turns out, his boss's father owned the house and it was the house that his boss had grown up in! To take things just one step further, his father not only knew my uncle, he was one of his friends!

A synchronistic flow of events, with each lining up perfectly behind the other, is part of manifesting miracles. Being willing to be "in the flow" with a feel-good energy just seems to connect all the pieces in unexpected ways. No struggles involved. Amusing at the very least, and fascinating to my soul. Many times I've remarked that I just "can't make this up." Somehow a cosmic interaction takes place, but first you must work with the Universe by asking, which puts you in the flow of receiving. Then, there are more action pieces of following where you are being led.

As you've already figured out, I did buy this home in that town where I didn't want to live. Truthfully, I have no idea what I'm doing here or how long I'll stay. I only know that for now, it is where I'm meant to be. Some inner wisdom tells me that there's something that needs to be healed within my ancestral lineage, and perhaps the area. I remain grateful every single day for the opportunity to grow and expand, as this property pushes me way outside my comfort zone. I'm learning how to be a good landlord, how to care for a home as a single woman, how to nurture the gardens, and how to be a good steward of the land.

Much to my surprise and delight, I'm also learning how to love this new community that's filled with days gone by, learning how to be *present* when there are so many memories of those beloved ones who've gone before me. Keeping love alive by remembering to remember to honor the ancestors and the lives they lived. At the same time, I must claim my own life. Celebrating the memories from a place of love, perhaps recognizing some of my own gifts and talents passed on to me through the generations. Moving forward, I'm acknowledging that though we are connected, I am different. I am unique and I deserve to live my own life in my own way.

Miracles! They surround each and every one of us--if we are only open to receiving them. I've learned to trust this invisible, creative, formless substance that is always communicating, allowing this Divine Energy Intelligence to work through me and with me in a partnership of co-creation. Even when my mind wants to tell me that I'm all alone, I know in my heart of hearts that is not the truth. All I need is a miracle!

Dedicated to my son Ian Daniel Tobey, my greatest teacher.

Thank you God for walking with me each and every day! Deep gratitude to my family and friends who fill my life with such JOY and many of my life's lessons. Each one of you are invaluable to the personal growth in my life, each one priceless! Special thanks to my brothers and my sister; Robert, Jim, Steve and Nancy who have each been there for me at different times throughout the years. There aren't the words to express the love I have for you. I appreciate the grace you extend by allowing me to simply be me…xoxo

~Donna Jutras Tobey

Tracy Carlson

TRACY CARLSON is a certified transformational life coach, as well as a registered social worker specializing in clinical counseling. She is an educator, mentor, counselor, program developer, speaker, workshop facilitator and author.

Tracy resides in Saskatoon, Saskatchewan, Canada, where she enjoys music, art, culture and meandering along the river trails. She loves spending time with her family, cuddling grandbabies, sharing belly laughs with friends, and engaging in conversations about things that matter with people who care.

tracy@outofthebluetherapy.ca
www.outofthebluetherapy.ca

Everyday Miracles

Ah, miracles. Those unexplained mystery gifts that seem to come out of the blue. As more and more people become aware of their ability to access a power that is greater than themselves—a higher knowing—it seems as if more miracles are being experienced in everyday lives.

> Miracles are like pimples, because once you start looking for them you find more than you ever dreamed you'd see.
>
> ~ LEMONY SNICKET, *The Lump of Coal*

However, spiritual growth is not always all unicorns and rainbows. Awakening to the truth of who you are and taking responsibility for the results you see in your life can—at first—feel as though the sky is falling. Deepak Chopra says that all great change is preceded by chaos, and I have found that chaos is often preceded by a broken heart.

Broken Hearts Let the Light in

I experienced my first broken heart when I was 10 years old. My parents had separated and my father moved to another province. Children tend to blame themselves when parents divorce, and I was no exception. However, I believed in forgiveness and miracles. I held on to the belief that my Dad would return home. In my imagination, I could hear his car pull up to the house. I could see him standing in the kitchen with the sun streaming through the window in the morning. I could smell bacon frying on the stove and hear my mom laughing at his silly jokes. I felt my heart sing with joy at the sight of his smiling, handsome face, scooping me up into a bear hug. When I told my mom about my vision and my belief, she said, "Don't build up your hopes." I wasn't the most obedient child, and her words inspired a deep resolve in me. I imagined my faith, hope and love were golden bricks, and I piled them up until they reached heaven. I allowed myself to believe.

Other broken hearts would find me over the years but none so painful as the one I experienced when my children left home. I had entered a phase of life that felt joyful, even exuberant. I began writing a book. I was inspired to start a life coaching business. Life was good.

However, it was like I had started running downhill. I went too fast, lost my footing and began a violent downward spiral that I couldn't seem to control. I sank into a depression so deep I could hardly function. For months I got up, went to work, came home, went to bed. The next day I would start again. I just wanted to die. Yet, in the midst of it I knew this was no ordinary depression; there was something deeper in it. The suffering was so intense that it really felt like a spiritual roto-rooting.

Down for the Count

I began an involuntary moral inventory that was far from fearless. Everything in my inner and outer life that no longer served me was rising up for surrender and release. I felt as though I had turned into mush. I could not find my shape. This was a dark night of the soul and I realized I was being called out.

No more hiding, no more playing small, no more playing the martyr or the damsel in distress. I was being called upon to step into the role of hero of my own story, to walk my talk, to take up my pen and "right" the life story of victimhood I had been reciting most of my life. I realized that I had been believing in lies about myself that had led me to living a muted, wounded life expression. I became determined to learn the lesson this dark night had come to teach.

I am NOT going through this for nothing. Something BIG is happening here!

I prayed, I studied, and I meditated. All I could do was hold the broken pieces of my heart and life up to God, to my Higher Self, to a power greater than me. I read the books that came to me. I talked to the people who came to me. I listened, listened, listened. *Here I am, God.* I was determined to remain willing, to surrender, to allow the process to unfold.

Just breathe.

Slowly I began to get better at sitting with pain, to get better at surrendering, and I began to forgive myself. I began to see clearly.

A Dark Night of the Soul

All of us go through a dark night at some point in our lives. A dark night serves as a crucible, burning away the parts of us that are no longer necessary, the parts we need to release in order to grow, the parts that hold us back. Old limiting beliefs, old habits that no longer serve us, relationships that have reached their season and are calling for release.

Dark nights often preclude an awakening of epic proportion, and if we accept them, if we are willing to sit with the chaos, a new normal begins to appear. A new life and way of being begins to emerge that is brighter, deeper and more fulfilling than we could ever imagine.

Here's what I now know about a dark night of the soul: when it descends upon you, REJOICE! It is a sign that greatness is seeking to emerge through you. New marching orders are at hand. Great peace and happiness await you on the other side of the pain. Declare victory and you will come to the realization that you don't want it to end too soon, because you want all that it has come to teach you.

The Miracle of Transformation

The caterpillar knows when it is time to spin a cocoon, enter a chrysalis stage and withdraw from the world for a time. We all know this, and we know that inside that cocoon, a miracle of transformation occurs. However, there are some things about this process you may not know.

Once inside the cocoon, the caterpillar's body begins to experience a complete breakdown of the physical form. It withdraws from the world as it knows it, and it turns to mush. Inside that mush, cells begin to appear that biologists call imaginal cells. The imaginal cells contain the blueprint of the butterfly.

At first, the caterpillar's immune system tries to destroy these cells, but they persist. They gently, persistently and calmly continue to appear and then they begin to communicate. They attract one another, congregate together and begin to multiply. In time the form of a butterfly is co-created. When the process of creation is complete, the butterfly begins to emerge from the chrysalis, and a new struggle begins.

It takes strength to emerge into the light.

A Teaching Story

A young woman is out walking in the woods when she comes across a beautiful butterfly emerging from its chrysalis. She watches in wonder as it struggles for freedom. Feeling compassion for the beautiful creature, she reaches down and gently helps it break free from its confines. The beautiful butterfly spreads out its wings to dry in the sunlight, but it soon becomes apparent that something is wrong. The butterfly is weak, it can't hold up its wings, and its body crumbles. The butterfly falls to the ground and dies.

The woman returns home, distraught, and relays her story to her husband. Her husband gently explains that the butterfly requires the struggle it takes to emerge from the chrysalis in order to enter into a new phase of being.

It is the struggle that makes it strong, it is the struggle that is the catalyst for vibrancy; it is the struggle that enables the butterfly to use its wings to take flight.

Crawl or Fly?

> You were born with wings, why do you prefer to crawl through the dirt? Learn to use your wings and fly!
>
> ~ RUMI

I wonder if the reason most of us prefer to crawl through the dirt is because of the unwillingness to embrace the struggle life sometimes presents us with. A death, a sickness, a divorce, a financial crisis; whatever lessons come to us contain blessings when we are willing to accept them.

Unwillingness to embrace the dark night of the soul and take what it has come to teach us prolongs our suffering, blinds us to the blessings in it and keeps us crawling through the dirt. Turning into mush and staying in the chrysalis where it's uncomfortable but safe can be tempting. Embracing a new normal, emerging into a bigger reality, growing and stretching into a new way of being requires a choice: faith or fear? Choosing fear dooms us to repeat the same lessons again and again.

Learning to be grateful IN it, not FOR it, is a great lesson. Gratitude opens the mind for a shift in perception, which in turn cultivates miracle mindedness. Dr. Wayne Dyer liked to say, "When you change the way you look at a thing, the thing you look at changes."

When we choose to surrender and turn our lives over to a force greater than us—the part that seeks ever fuller, more free, expanded expression of life—then we trust those imaginal cells of creation to go to work and show us a life of deep and profound meaning and good purpose. We nurture a mindset that welcomes miracles in every form.

When I was 15 years old, I dreamed that I heard the crunch of gravel as my father's car turned into our driveway. My parents had been divorced for almost 5 years and I had seen him just once in all that time. I wrote him letters; I kept him calmly in my prayers, knowing he was only ever a thought away. I kept tending my imaginal brick wall of faith, hope and love, seeing it shining golden in the sun, solidly stretching up to heaven. I sat with a quiet knowing in my heart that he would someday return home.

The morning that I dreamed I had heard his car in the driveway, I awoke to strange voices in the kitchen, a man's voice, and my mother's laughter. I could see golden sunshine streaming in through my bedroom window. I could smell bacon frying on the stove. I entered the kitchen, and there he was.

Three months later my parents remarried and this year they celebrated their 56th wedding anniversary.

Nurture your imaginal cells. Choose faith, love madly, and everyday expect miracles.

Dedicated to my three extraordinary children, Chantal, Juste and Braden and to my beautiful, brilliant grandchildren, Kaya, Annabel and Elizabeth. All of you are my miracles, my special gifts from God, and I love you to the moon and back.

Thank you to every Soul who shares my journey, past, present and future. Special gratitude to those who help me excavate my inner gifts: Ron Dupuis, surrender. Jonathon Fonos, strength. Phyllis Paterson, perspective. Ann Dupuis, discernment. Yvonne Houston, unconditional love. Brenda Fedorchuk, wisdom. Thank you to my spiritual and business mentors, Mary Morrissey and Heather Dominick for your inspiration to get real, get honest, and get on with it. Thank you to my brilliant editor, Braden Dupuis. Thank you to my sister Tricia Carlson Lucyshyn for lending your wings to me when mine were broken. Love, love, love you all.

-Tracy Carlson

Trish Bowie

TRISH BOWIE searched for a miracle after serious loss, illness and years of pain. She found her miracle at the age of 39 when she was introduced to Reiki Energy Healing and Louise Hay's wonderful book *Heal Your Body.* In 1996 she became a Usui Reiki Master—then continued with Reiki training and obtained her Karuna, Shamballa, Jikiden, and Divine Compassion Masters. She is a Registered Massage Therapist, Certified Hypnotherapist and a Certified and Licensed **Heal Your Life®** Teacher. Trish is owner of The Complete Wellness Centre and Day Spa, and The Western Canada Reiki Training Centre, offering workshops for teens and adults in Usui, Karuna and Shamballa Reiki, **Heal Your Life®**, Stress Management, Money Awareness, Divine Compassion, Energy Effects, Meditation and Spa Training. She feels very honored to have had the opportunity to learn from so many great leaders and Masters. Trish is humbled and grateful for the ability to facilitate people to heal.

reikitraining@gmail.com
www.thecompletewellnesscentre.com

Moving Beyond The Unknown

After growing up and living in the city throughout my childhood years, and then moving to the country, I quickly discovered what it was like to have lots of people around me while still feeling so alone and terrified, like a caged animal pacing up and down with no escape in sight.

I fell in love and was married at the age of 19. A year later I had my first child. A son. Eight months after he was born my husband wanted to leave the city I grew up in to move closer to his family in Northern Alberta Canada. It was his dream to go back home within five years of having our son. Imagine how I felt when he came home a few months later instead and said, *"We are moving."*

Parts of me were excited and a part of me was really scared to take on this new adventure. Moving to the bush, four long hours away from home, away from my family, the city lights, my security! It was so completely different from what I was accustomed to. We had everything we could ever want in the city and I loved it there. I simply had to hop on a bus if I wanted to go anywhere and we always had enough money to do what we wanted.

I loved fashion, theater, and the endless attractions the city could offer me... and my family. I loved my family! Now here we were packing up all of our belongings and moving to the bush. No buses, no restaurants, no fashion, no running water, no money. My husband quit his job so he could go help his Dad, who had been injured by a horse that rolled on top of him. So there I was saying goodbye to my beautiful city—wide-eyed and ready to do whatever it was I needed to do to learn survival. It seemed exciting because we were going to rent a house on some land after living in an apartment in the city. I felt so free.

Life in the Bush...

The house was a good size and I did my best to make it look nice with the furnishings we'd brought from the city. The living room felt very cozy and inviting with my red shag carpet and red lamps. It had a bay window, from which I hung lace curtains, and they looked wonderful! The couple who rented it to us really loved what I had done. In a short time though I started to feel the negative effects of our decision ... we had no running water, which meant we had to catch rain or use melted snow, and heat the water to do the dishes. Then there were the dirty diapers that had to be washed by hand! Going outside to the outhouse in the middle of winter was not fun either!

There were a few other things that were really difficult for me to deal with ... like that little hole in the kitchen wall, which looked like the door to a mouse house on TV. Well it became my reality because mice did indeed scurry in and out of there. I had nightmares that they were crawling all over me in bed at night, which they very well may have been. Then there was the other issue ... the one about the owner having a key and coming in the back entrance of the house where there was a table with chairs to have his lunch—unannounced. I found out the hard way. One day I ran to the fridge, which was right next to that room, to get the baby a bottle ... without a stitch on and there he was! I was so embarrassed. I just wanted to go home.

Since we had no money I couldn't easily pick up the phone and telephone my family. It was so expensive to call long distance back in the late 1970's—and we were on a party line where at least 3 homes shared the same line, so you never said anything that you didn't want people to know because sure as heck someone would be listening. I was starting to feel the stress and was pregnant with my perfectly-planned second child. That fun, exciting place wasn't so much fun anymore. The strain of having no money was weighing heavily on us. We lived on $3,200 that year and when we didn't eat at the in-laws, we ate at home where it was eggs, rice, peas and canned corned beef. I was pretty skinny and my nutrition wasn't the best, so I lost my second baby and I was devastated. I truly wanted that baby. I cried for days ... feeling confined and no longer free.

I had to get out of there. I ran outside to get away, up and down the driveway like a caged animal with nowhere to go, no vehicle, no money, no phoning home ... It was at that moment that I began learning how to suppress my pain, how to pretend to be happy, how to be the Super Mom and Wife, and how to please everyone but myself. I went willingly to the north, so now I had to live with it.

Just When the Clouds Seem to Lift...

A year later I was pretty excited when my husband gave me the good news that his aunt was going to give us money for a down payment on one of the old forestry station houses that had running water! I was so excited! I swore I would never have another dirty dish. My husband and his brother decided they would start a land survey business together. Everything seemed great, since I was pregnant once again and I could actually wash diapers in a washing machine this time.

The house was a three-bedroom home on 4 acres and we had a water dugout which was our drinking supply. We bought three hundred and twenty acres of homestead land, as well as one hundred and sixty acres of farmed land across the road from our house that belonged to my father-in-law. My husband taught me how to disc the field after the baby was born. When it was dark at night and while sitting on that big tractor, I felt so independent, so in control. I was really starting to enjoy the country life as my husband continued to teach me the love of the land.

Then came that horrible day in June.... My husband decided to get out his dad's boat and bluestone the dugout. Bluestone (copper sulfate) was used to kill the algae in the water. So he and our four-year-old son set out to get the job done. It was a beautiful, peaceful day. The sun was shining and warming every part of my body as I sat in the yard playing with my 14-month-old daughter. My husband and son were in the boat rowing around the dugout with the bag of bluestone hanging from the boat, dissolving into the water and doing its job.

"Mom!" shouted my son from the boat. *"Can I please have some juice?"* I had my husband bring him to the bank of the dugout and I took him into the house for juice. We continued to enjoy the warmth as we sat and chatted about his ride in the boat.

I suddenly heard a funny sound coming from the area of the dugout—a grunting noise and lots of splashing. I ran over towards the dugout only to find my husband frantic in the water with the boat flipped over. He swam over to the boat while I searched around for a rope to throw out to him. The first thing I saw was a garden hose. I grabbed it and ran over to the bank. For some reason he wasn't hanging on to the boat. I was later informed it had hit him in the head and stunned him! He was in the middle of the dugout with his back turned to me and bobbing up and down. I quickly took off some of my clothes and jumped in to try to save him. When I got to where he was, he was inexplicably gone. Family and friends came right away and jumped in looking for him. The R.C.M.P. (Royal Canadian Mounted Police) were contacted. A diver came in and one hour later his body was recovered.

I was in a state of shock. There I was in the bush with a four-year-old and a fourteen-month-old. No Last Will from my husband, no money for the first three months, no driver's license, thirty miles to the closest town—all at the young age of twenty-four.

I knew one thing. I had to grow up fast. The man I was dependent upon was gone. I had two children that I needed to parent and I had to keep a smile on my face to ease their anxiety and pain. As I continued to suppress my grief, my body started to fight back. First I had back surgery, then my gall bladder came out, then the next year it was my appendix, then I started showing signs of fibromyalgia, then asthma …

Miracles Happen …

I met my present husband a few months after my husband drowned. He was new to the community, single and very nice. After a while he won me over and it was not difficult for me to fall in love again. Five years later we married and had a son together.

I recognized that I wanted to be somebody, to make a difference in the world because of the pain I had personally experienced. I started utilizing one of the artistic modalities I had found at a nearby college where I studied native cultural arts. I had always admired their ability to take something natural and make something beautiful with it.

I very successfully launched a business selling Canadian aboriginal fish scale art to members of government for dignitary gifts and hooked up with a company that marketed native art worldwide. Around the same time, I joined a cosmetic home-based business in order to help women feel better about themselves.

The thing I loved most about the company was their conventions. It was there that I started to hear positive people speaking and teaching. The more I heard the more I felt my own sadness and pain—and I knew I wanted to be positive like they were. I was feeling so physically drained though, and in such constant pain, that I frankly couldn't figure out how to get there.

It seemed like there were an unusual amount of tragedies happening within a few miles of where we lived. I felt such a heavy weight on my shoulders and I realized it was time for us to leave. To my surprise, my husband agreed. We packed up the family and moved to Central Alberta, conveniently one hour away from my family in the city. I was delighted.

Unfortunately, I continued to get ill and experience more debilitating pain. It seemed like I was becoming allergic to everything in life. It got so bad that each night before I went to bed, I would tell my husband specifically what was wrong with me, because I truly believed that I wasn't going to wake up in the morning and I wanted him to know what to tell the examining doctor after I died.

Eventually, I ended up in the hospital because I could not even lift a cup of coffee. The doctor was concerned that I had Guillain-Barre Syndrome. When acute, this condition can be life threatening and can affect the breathing muscles, so they were checking my respirations every 15 minutes.

An Awakening ...

That night as I laid there so afraid and wondering what was happening to my body, I felt an enormous stream of warmth go through the top of my head, down my body and out my toes. The word "stress" came into my mind and I perceived that was exactly what was causing my symptoms. The next morning, I informed the doctor and he told me that I needed to change my life or I could end up in a wheelchair.

As time went on, I returned to the hospital a few more times with various illnesses. I knew I had to do something different. I was released from hospital after being on intravenous fluid therapy.

I phoned a friend to come and give me a massage. She came over and said it's not a massage that you need, what you need is Reiki. She explained that Reiki worked on the physical, emotional, mental and spiritual body. I had refused it before. This time I was ready. I was so ill that I was willing to try anything. I was truly amazed! That one treatment had given me enough energy to get up and make a huge meal for my family.

I quickly understood that I had to learn how to do this ancient healing art so that I could help others the way I had been helped! I took the training and ultimately I was laying my hands on anyone who was willing to try this therapy. I couldn't get enough of it, so I went on to take my Masters in Reiki.

I treated myself daily and discovered I no longer needed to have a second back surgery. I also had no fibromyalgia symptoms. I went off my two asthma inhalers, as well. Around that time, I heard of a wonderful little book called ***Heal Your Body*** by Louise L. Hay. It taught about finding your illness, understanding the probable cause, and then developing a positive affirmation to heal it.

Every day I would go for a walk and say *"I'm stronger and stronger every day. I'm healthier and healthier in every way!"* Subsequently I felt amazing, like I was floating on a cloud. I noticed that I had a lot of control over my thoughts, and whenever I thought positively, it made a huge difference in the way my body felt.

Manifesting My Destiny...

I made sure to give myself a Reiki treatment every morning. Later, I started to meditate and continued saying my affirmations daily. I was so excited that I was healing myself. Now it was time for me to touch lives.

Twenty years ago I started teaching Reiki, as well as meditation. Sixteen years ago I opened a storefront that offered a Wellness Centre and Day Spa, as well as a training centre. It was an 800 sq. ft. building and we presented a variety of wellness and spa services. It was nice, but I comprehended that I wanted something bigger—so we could offer even more. There was a quaint place twice the size on the next block.

One day as I was walking by, I muttered to myself… *I wish you would move out so I could move in.*

The next day to my surprise the renters had moved out at midnight! It was then I realized that I could manifest precisely how busy I wanted things to be, how many gift certificates I wanted to sell at Christmas, even when I wanted things to change within the business. I became aware that my thoughts were powerful and they could make a definitive difference in my life. I continued to manifest my dreams and realities there for another 12 years. I loved the storefront, although it was not allowing me to live my dream to its fullest potential.

It has been quite exciting to touch so many lives and meet a myriad of wonderful souls along the way. In 2012 I decided I wanted to do even more and touch more lives. I recognized it was time for me to move my wellness centre and training centre to the country. It was peaceful there and I grasped that it was exactly what I and my clients needed.

I knew that in order to teach large groups of people how to heal and to be able to have time to write, I would need to close the storefront. It has been over three years. All that I focus on manifesting continues to become a reality. No matter what comes at me in my day-to-day life, I see it now as a gift. A gift to take me deeper into my spirituality… to explore who I am and how I can change my perception of that moment. A gift that shows me how to continue to create miracles in my life.

I am so grateful for every lesson, every ounce of pain and illness, as well as for my losses, for they have taught me to be strong, courageous and forgiving.

To my husband who has so willingly supported me on my journey, my children who teach me to love daily, my grandchildren for their precious wisdom, to my beautiful siblings for their unconditional love and to my friends, clients and students. God Bless you all!

I want to thank Louise L. Hay for her brilliance, and my other teachers and masters, too numerous to mention. Bruce Lipton for the encouragement to never give up on writing, my sister in-law Kim who saw the spark in me before I did! To my dearest friend Marg who kept me nourished, while I wrote and to God and my angels for continuing to support me.

-Trish Bowie

Deborah Bates

DEBORAH BATES was born and raised in Maine and has spent her life seeking spirit. She is a creator of songs, stories and magic, whether through her writing or her healing clairvoyant work. She brings her life experiences and wisdom as a woman living across the expanse of this country, raising two sons, and honoring her ties to all creatures on this earth into her work as a mystic healer. She resides in the Santa Cruz Mountains, on the edge of the Pacific, continuing her deep connection to the ocean and its surrounding life.

www.DebbyBates.com

Messenger of the Light

The call came at four o'clock in the morning. I had been expecting it. I heard the concern in my sister-in-law's voice, *"Debby, Elliott is in the hospital and he's dying. It's time to come home."* My Dad was ninety years old and had slowly been losing his strength over the past year to congestive heart failure. He had been living with my younger brother, Daniel, in his home in Kennebunkport, Maine. Two days earlier at four in the morning I had woken up out of a sound sleep. My body shot up so that I was sitting straight up in my bed and I sang *By the Rivers of Babylon* at full volume. Then I immediately lay back down and fell asleep. I had a premonition of what was to come.

After the phone call, I got up, booked a flight and began to pack my suitcase. As I walked around and around my cabin preparing for this journey to say goodbye to my father, I was suddenly sucked up into a spiral of energy. The vortex was so strong that I had no choice. I don't remember leaving my body, but I felt compressed on all sides while I was being pulled up into the light. As I twirled through pinks and blues, I heard music so sweet I thought that my heart would burst. I remember feeling the most intense ecstasy and peace that I have ever known. In the distance I heard myself laughing and crowing with joy and delight. There was a roaring hum, but I didn't hear any of the usual sounds from my home. I didn't have any thoughts except that I knew I was not in control.

I have no idea how much time went by, but after experiencing this blissful eternity I was suddenly slammed onto a hard surface. I looked down and saw my feet firmly planted on the green painted plywood floor by the ladder to my loft. Though stunned, I was still filled with delight. I started dancing around my cabin, laughing and singing. I could smell the sharp acrid singe of my coffee on the stove, and slowly the room came back to me. *What just happened? Oh well, it doesn't matter. I just need to pack.* I floated around gathering my things for the trip and somehow was packed and ready when I heard the crunch of tires on the gravel outside as my friend arrived to drive me through the mountains to the San Jose Airport. When we were cruising over Highway 17, my cell phone power came on and I saw that I had a message. It was from my brother telling me that Dad had died. I let this sink in as my friend drove me to the airport. While sitting in the plane flying over the Rockies, I realized that at the same time I was spinning in the vortex and flying into the light my dad had just died. It struck me to the core of my being that I was the one who had carried him over to the Other Side. A few days earlier I had asked Daniel to hold Dad while he was dying if I couldn't make it back home to his bedside in time. Later, Daniel shared with me that he had been with him, keeping a hand on his shoulder talking to him as he passed... "Dad, here we are. It looks like this is it and we're here together." A nurse later walked in and told Daniel he could stop talking now. Elliott had died. Daniel and I each had done our job. He comforted our father's body in his last moments while I carried our dad home to the Other Side.

When Daniel told me how afraid Elliott was to die, I was reminded of a night back in 1954 when I woke up in my bed and couldn't move my body. I cried out for my parents, lying there, not understanding why I had no feeling in my legs and back. It was a long night as we went to the local hospital and I was admitted with polio. I was so afraid, but I remember how safe I felt when my Dad wrapped me up in a blanket and carried me in his arms to the car and then onto the children's ward of Central Maine General Hospital. I felt his care and love as I made the transition to my stay there. Now here I was returning the love by helping him when he was so afraid to leave this world. My years of training as a clairvoyant healer allowed me to take this role in his life. I know that all of this was orchestrated long before my birth.

It's been five years now since Dad died. The other day as I sat in meditation, Dad's spirit appeared and let me know that I was to go on a journey with him. He wanted to show me what he had learned and places of interest to him on the Other Side. He also had some Ascended Masters that he wanted me to meet. His spirit showed up to me as a cherub messenger, full of child-like enthusiasm and joy. I saw him as he looked in an old photograph at ten years old, standing by the side of a tide pool, sailing his model boat, The Nautilus. He reminded me of Peter Pan, as we soared up through the Astral to the place where spirits play in eternity. We flew beyond The Healing Temple and passed the doorways to many levels of the celestial plane. First he showed me where he had arrived upon his death, to meet God. At the blue door he stopped and told me I do not have to go in right now. After that we turned back and went to the Threshold to a room where he had cleared family karma from this lifetime. We flew through corridors and were greeted by many spirits. My Dad was proud to show me around and let me see this world, as he knew it.

He is free now. His immense grief is gone. He no longer holds the guilt and shame of lifetimes and is happy to be his true spirit. I noticed as we were flying how alike we are. I am doing much of the karmic clearing down here that he did after he arrived at God's door. He led me down a path to my Council; there were three members sitting at a huge table. They stood up and started clapping when we walked in. They were laughing and slapping Dad on the back. He had done his job. They all know that I get turned around and easily lost which is why Dad was assigned to take me through the different spiritual stations and up to meet them. Dad was my anchor when he was alive but that job is being passed on to another during this journey. While on earth he had provided for me financially, but emotionally and spiritually he couldn't show up. I had to fill in those parts myself. It was in seeking my spiritual truth and healing my emotional body that I was shown the way to hold my father and take him over to God.

As we said our true good bye, Dad stepped to the side. His work with me was now over. I felt so much love for him as we parted. It took his passing to heal our relationship, which had been broken during his lifetime as my father. The healing had to happen in death and beyond. My spirit gets to return to earth and each day let people know that the miracle of great healing can always occur, even if a loved one has died. We just have to be willing to go within and fly towards the light.

Dedicated to my father, Elliott Maxcy Bates. I am so grateful that we got to share in the spirit world.

I have much gratitude for my brother Dr. Daniel Bates who with his wife Daphne Pulsifer took care of Elliott in their home during his last few years in life.

Huge thank you to my brother John Bates for taking care of business so graciously.

Blessings to my sister Susan Eddy for holding the northern point of our family star.

-Deborah Bates

Mimi Tran

MIMI TRAN is a day spa business owner, life coach, workshop leader, motivational speaker, ballroom dancer, author—and a believer and dreamer.

She resides in East Brunswick, New Jersey, where she enjoys and shares her miraculous journey with two amazing teen daughters, her mother, family and friends. She loves to travel to different places for leisure, as well as to give motivational speeches, workshops, and to life coach. Mimi's passion is to serve and inspire others to create the reality that they desire to live, and/or enhance it in any way possible. She embraces her remarkable life story and uses this enthusiasm to fuel her passion every day.

Mimitran26@yahoo.com

 Believe In Yourself

It was the year 1980—five years after the Vietnam War ended. The communists had taken over. Our world was controlled by a totalitarian government. If you had a house, they took it away from you. If you had money, they took that too. They would send all of the rich people, who had accumulated wealth during the war, to a camp where they had to work very hard for only two meals a day. It was the punishment for being wealthy.

I was born and raised in Saigon, the New York City of Vietnam. But, even though we lived in such an extravagant city, my family was not rich. As a matter of fact, we didn't have much at all. My mother had some savings that she accrued during the war, but we could not last long without decent jobs. Forget about decent. There was no such thing as a decent job. Just a job if you were lucky.

We found out the U.S. Government opened up to take in children from the war to America. My father was an American soldier, so I was one of those kids. We applied through the O.D.P., the Orderly Departure Program, created by the U.S. Government just for us. However, because there were so many war children like me, rumors spread that the legal process could take 10 plus years, if you didn't know the right channels through the Vietnamese Offices. We were happy with the opportunity, but so discouraged with the rumor. With the little saving we had left, we were afraid we wouldn't last until that day came. My mother couldn't wait that long.

So, after five years of struggling for survival, life was getting tougher and tougher every day to make ends meet. My mother decided to take the first (and last) chance that we could afford to escape the country. She used up all of her savings to pay for two seats on a tiny wooden boat to illegally leave Vietnam. Since it was an illegal escape, the whole operation was very secretive. My mother and I waited patiently for over two months, hiding out at a friend's house by the water at different locations and different times.

The operation failed. We never even got to the boat. The government found out about it and terminated it immediately. They were waiting at the dock so they could catch us and throw us in jail. Even though we didn't escape the country, at least we escaped the police and avoided imprisonment.

We lost all of our money and came back home only to be broke and still jobless.

My mother stayed back at a friend's place in Saigon to start over with next to nothing and focus on the O.D.P. application process. And me? Since I had not been to school for so long, the school would not admit me back. I got kicked out of elementary school after being absent for over two months and I was never allowed to go back to finish 5*th* grade.

A Miraculous Gift

After that, I realized that the small, crowded Saigon city did not have anything to offer me. My mother and I decided that I had to go and stay with my grandmother and my aunt to help them with their farm at a town called Binh Chuan, about 30 miles from Saigon.

I remember, the very first day my aunt took me to the farm, I was terrified with the amount of work that needed to be done on this giant piece of land we had. Since the last harvest, needle bushes had grown like weeds on every single inch of the place. Our job was to cut each of them from the root, let them dry, burn them, and get the land ready for the planting season. The entire farm was completely covered in those bushes, and we'd have to work through all of it.

There were no such things as "gloves," so getting poked and bleeding from those needles was naturally expected. The work seemed so overwhelming, I started to cry and I couldn't stop. My aunt thought that I had stepped on one of those needle bushes and got hurt, therefore, she told me to be careful and showed me how to get around them. I couldn't help but cry more. I didn't want to start the work. My aunt asked again, "What is wrong?"

I sobbed, "The farm is so big, there are so many needle bushes to cut, and only two of us. How are we ever going to get it done?" She smiled and calmly comforted me.

She said "Oh honey, think like this ... It doesn't matter how big or small the job is ... It doesn't matter if you choose to do the job or you must do the job ... It doesn't matter if you cry and drain more energy through the job and take longer to finish or you learn to like the job ... embrace it with your enthusiasm and finish the job faster. When you finish the job you will feel great accomplishment, instead of relief that the punishment is over. Besides, we have no money to hire someone else to help us. So, this is all on us and up to us to decide how we want to do this." I wiped off my tears and we got to work.

At the end of each day, we looked at what we had finished and celebrated instead of worrying about what was not done. Eventually, we finished sooner than we expected. Little did I know, that was one of the most valuable lessons I would ever learn in my lifetime.

After that, every time I was faced with any task, I looked back on what my aunt said and then I knew what to do. I applied this lesson throughout my life, whether it was cleaning my house, or opening a new business. I have grown from "Why me?" to "Thank you."

Every day on the farm, I looked up in the sky and each time an airplane flew by, I told myself, one day I will be on that plane up there, flying to America to start my American dream journey. That was my only hope and goal: to be something in this lifetime. Otherwise, I probably would have gotten married at fifteen years old, had three kids by eighteen and been the servant for my husband's family for the rest of my days. The alternative was unthinkable for me.

Fast Forward Five Years

I was 15 years old. We finally got the news that we could leave through the O.D.P. by airplane to go to America, free of charge and all inclusive! Really! It was a dream come true for me. It was like I had lived only for this day to come and it was finally here. The feeling of joy was nearly suffocating. Everything else didn't matter. I was going to America. Woo-hoo! Ready or not... here I come.

We left Vietnam on Halloween, October 31st, 1985.

After a long process of stopping in Bangkok, Thailand's Refugee camp for three weeks and then, Bataan, Philippine's Refugee Camp for six months for some more paperwork and learning about English and the American's society, we finally arrived at Binghamton, NY, late at night on May 31st, 1986.

I came to America with a dream, a mission to be accomplished. That was to get an education. I knew I missed 5 years of school. I knew I spoke only broken English. Nevertheless, I also seemed to have exactly what I needed. And that was determination, hard work, and a never-give-up attitude.

The years I spent on the farm had taught me many things about who I am. Because I had to endure those hardships at such a young age, I built up my tolerance, discipline and accountability. I learned to love and embrace my journey, to be patient about what I could and could not change. The more I learned, the closer my dream felt to me. That was what helped me on the farm. Who would have thought that all the years that I couldn't wait to pass had prepared me to help make my dream come true? I now realized I was exactly where I was supposed to be.

Reality hit me immediately the very next day after I arrived, when my sponsor came to visit us at our studio apartment and tried to have a conversation with me. I couldn't understand him much. I tried to reply to some of the things I could pick up on, but the man couldn't understand me either. The very first English conversation I had with an American was much more frustrating than exciting. Especially, when I thought that I had six months of English under my belt and that I was ready to get to work. Obviously, I was not.

My apartment happened to be in the same building as my childhood friend. She shared with me that she had the same problem a year earlier when she first got here. I had tried to learn as much vocabulary as possible. But because I learned English in the Philippines by Filipino teachers, my English had a strong accent: English + Filipino accent + Vietnamese accent = *Gibberish*

And that was a problem. But I had a solution. I immediately signed up for the local summer E.S.L. (English as a Second Language) class.

Summer seemed to last forever, but when Fall finally arrived I was extremely excited. After all those years of waiting and dreaming, I was actually going to a "real school"—High School. Because of my age, my improving English, and all the help from my E.S.L. teacher, I was able to negotiate with my guidance counselor to let me start in 10th grade instead of 9th. I never told anyone at the school that I'd never finished elementary school, that I never knew what middle school was like and that I'd never even started 9th grade. I had no knowledge of math, biology, history, or art. I just signed up for what my childhood friend signed up for.

That was very upsetting for her. She came to the U.S. one year before me. She never missed school like I did and her education background was solid. She had even studied English for many years in Vietnam before going to America. Therefore, she decided that there was no way that I could be in the same grade as she was. I should have at least been one grade behind. I didn't agree with that. I made it clear to her that I came a very long way to get here and that there was no way anyone or anything was going to push me back now.

Even though I had no idea what I had signed up for, I believed I could do it, I wanted to do it, and I had to do this.

The counselor was very uncertain about putting me in 10th grade, so I made a deal with him. If I passed all my courses in the first semester, then he had to allow me to stay in 10th grade. If I didn't make the cut, I would have to go back to 9th to start over. It was a win/win situation for me, given my situation. I just wanted to finish high school as soon as possible, so I could go to college. I was in a hurry to get my mission accomplished. He agreed. I remembered leaving his office and telling him, "I am not going to 9th grade."

He said, "Good luck!"

Manifesting My Dream

I worked nights and days and passed that 1st semester. I finished high school in three years and got my bachelor's degree four years after that. The reason I was able to keep going was because I believed in myself.

I didn't have any time to sit there and question the choices I'd made. I never used the excuse of having broken English or missing five years of school. I never complained that it was too difficult. Instead, I was so grateful for the opportunity to make a change and improve my circumstances. Besides, I was way too busy studying to make any excuses.

Every school day I got home, had a little bit to eat and started on my homework. Most of the time, I had to stay up until 2 AM just to translate my homework using a dictionary in order to find out what it meant before I could actually do it. Sometimes, even after translating everything, I still had no idea what it was asking me. I have to say, my E.S.L. teacher was a God-sent angel. She tried to understand my wishes and dreams in any way she possibly could, but you can see why it would be difficult for her. She would ask me, "Why are you in such a hurry?"

I'd reply, "I am five years behind with no English background, I've got no time to catch up and I got to go to college, find a good job and have a better life!"

My supposed-friend from childhood (the first friend I met in America and the only friend I had in school) constantly told me how hard it was, how I should have started in 9th grade, how I should go back to 9th grade, how I would never make it and so on. I used her words as my jumping off point, my *trampoline*. The more she tried to push me back, the further I wanted to go ahead and the higher I wanted to jump. I was grateful for her friendship—in an untraditional way.

My mission in America was to get an education so I could improve life for myself and my family... even though I had no idea what I was signing up for. But I believed, if there is a will, there is always a way. So I just focused on how to get it. I had no time to think about how hard it was. I was too busy learning (and I still am).

My old dream was to create a better life, but now, I have a wonderful life. A life, full of love, gratitude, harmony, peace, and fun with my children. And the reward is breathtaking whenever I can find the opportunity to make a positive impact on someone's experience through my journey and life coaching.

I am where I am today, not because of what I have accumulated through the years, but because of what I have learned and because I have never stopped learning.

My past experiences have helped me tremendously in so many ways. They have shaped me into the woman I am. I love life and myself. I challenge my potential every day. I embrace each and every moment of this incredible path because, as we all know, it will never come by again.

Dedicated to Jessica and Celina. This universe has only one sun and one moon. I am blessed with two of each.

Thanks to Lisa Hardwick for this amazing opportunity. Thanks to Dung Tran (my aunt) for the life lessons and stories on the farm. Thanks to my children for their inspiration, love and non-stop support. Thanks to my mother for being the best teacher. Thanks to the Nirvana Team for carrying out my vision. And thanks to the Nirvana fans, for the love and continue support.

-Mimi Tran

Vandana Mendonca

Soul Miracles is VANDANA MENDONCA'S second foray in the literary world of collaborative writing. Her first being the insightful *Potential Me*, in *The Empowerment Manual*. Her ultimate dream is to share her knowledge on a world-wide stage.

Vandana is a highly skilled and intuitive Holistic Wellness Specialist and Trainer. Her unique approach addresses the 'Whole; Mind, Body & Spirit,' and the connection that influences the condition. Her role in this process is one of Therapist, Mentor and Wellness Coach. She is passionate about a pragmatic application of spirituality in everyday life and in the self-fulfillment process. Her forte is connecting with Angels.

Vandana.mendonca@yahoo.com,
www.facebook.com/Vandanahealthnharmony/
http://www.amazon.com/Vandana-Mendonca/e/B017OF2Z60/ref=ntt_dp_epwbk_9

Soul Miracles

The Leap Of Faith

Committing to a chapter in *The Manifestation of Modern Miracles* was a huge leap of faith for me. There was nothing defining for me to write about or so I thought, yet I was confident that I had much to share. My life has been a collection of beautiful synchronistic events some of which have manifested into what I interpret with the benefit of hindsight as miracles, little and large. I am ever grateful for the messages I am given, as well as for the lessons learned as a consequence. It is my belief that in the greater scheme of things, our lives are all intertwined, so as you read on don't be surprised to draw parallels in your own life.

Perhaps I wasn't sure if the miracles on my mind were profound enough and worthy of sharing. This hesitancy prompted me to turn to my all-time favorite process of seeking answers from my spirit guides. I do this when I need greater clarity on any aspect of life in general and for the many questions I have about the spiritual laws of the Universe. I wasn't born with the natural ability to connect with spirit guides but I have learned how and have become adept simply by working at it with an open mind and understanding the responses.

"I know not what lies beyond, my faith in heaven above.
Through the open door I step, my heart is filled with love."

The Ritual

So I sat down on my meditation cushion, yes I have one. Well it's an ordinary cushion that I feel very comfy sitting on in daily meditation. I held on to my meditation crystals. I call them my meditation crystals because they help me connect. Different strokes for different folks and you may or may not feel the need of a crystal. It's whatever you are happy with. I know people who like meditating with a plant nearby and I can see the logic in that. Do what helps you connect.

I have pen and paper handy so that a record of messages can be made while they are still fresh in the mind. I have learned to recognize these messages as gifts from the Universe and I alluded to this in my previous collaborative effort, 'The Empowerment Manual; Potential Me.'

The next step was for me to state my intention. I did this in my mind and asked that they reveal to me the words and images to shape the direction of this chapter. The first image was one of "Fire," not a raging or destructive fire but one that seemed to emit from within. The visual then manifested into the words "Burning desire to be recognized." Needing more clarity, I asked "Is this burning desire mine?" and "Yes" came the answer. That's when my conscious mind stepped in with a logical "Hey, I didn't even know I felt this way." With practise and an open mind the process gets easier and from experience I knew something needed to be addressed. I had to get to the root of this "Burning desire to be recognized" conundrum. In my meditative state I let myself be guided to the mystery behind the message.

The Explanation

So there I was, a little 8-year-old girl, happy in my own space but shy, almost wary of outsiders. I had a petite frame with amazing long and lustrous hair for which I was remembered more than for the person I was. Progressively, teachers knew me as the younger sibling of my very intelligent and high achieving sister. I have to smile at the memory of being constantly asked how come I wasn't like her. Oh well, go figure!

Even back then I had a love of dance and I am now a classically trained Bharat Natyam dancer, no doubt inspired by the dreams of an 8-year-old. But at the time all I wanted to do was dance with the freedom of the young at heart and perhaps influenced by the entertaining Bollywood dance style, full of emotion, fun and fashion all packaged in one. If my 8-year-old self could see me now I am sure she would smile and give me an enthusiastic thumbs-up for living a free-spirited life and true to the calling of my higher-self.

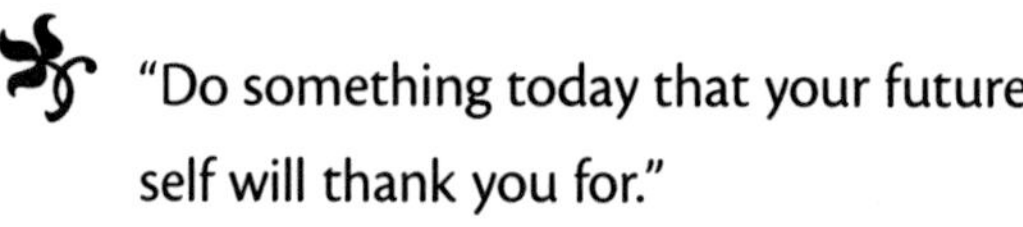

~ AUTHOR UNKNOWN

Fast forward to my life as a Holistic Therapist and I was shown the personally unique and intuitive methods I have been using over the years to help others heal. The prime one being what I was guided to call 'Grace Point Healing.'

The Realisation

I realized this was about my higher-self being present even as a child guiding me to this phase of my life without me being consciously aware of it. My second realization was about honoring 'Grace Point Healing' and introducing the concept on a public platform through this chapter. These 'aha' moments are pretty addicting for me as they put me into a state of raised awareness and sets my spirit soaring. These are my 'Soul Miracles,' simple, yet so very profound and enriching.

"Blessed am I to explore, and accept the inexplicable.
In my heart and soul I know, I manifest my own miracle."

Grace Point Healing

I won't go deep into an explanation as Grace Point Healing is still being refined. Nevertheless, here is a brief look at my approach.

- I first identify intuitively the individual's unique energy pattern. This includes their Spiritual, Physical, Emotional, Mental, Sub-Conscious, Ego and finally the Converging Point.
- To bring about balance I run the energy like a wave connecting all points.
- I then identify intuitively the individual's Primary and Secondary Endocrine Glands where any imbalances usually manifest the most.
- Finally, I plan the most appropriate therapy to integrate into Grace Point Healing.

I am pleased to share with you my personal intuitive guide on the Endocrine Glands and their connection with the personality. Using this I am able to support the individual and to empower them in their own self-healing process.

ENDOCRINE GLAND	PERSONAL IDENTITY	UNIVERSAL IDENTITY	EMOTIONAL INFLUENCER
Pituitary	Thinker	Creator/Inventor	Wanting Diversity or Change
Pineal	Seeker of Inner Peace	Philosopher	A Sense of Belonging
Thyroid	Expression	Communicator	To be Appreciated
Parathyroid	Stability	Balance/Enhancer	Growth & Strength
Thymus	Protector	Preserver	Feeling Safe & Secure
Pancreas	Assimilator/ Sustainer	Energizer	Fulfilling Potential
Adrenal	Go-Getter	Doer/Pioneer	Goal & Success Oriented
Reproductive	Contributor	Support/Developer	Responsible Involvement

Manifesting Through Meditation

Meditation is my vehicle for manifestation. What about you? Do you have something you call your own? I want to emphasize that we deserve good things in our lives. Some of them will happen through natural order. Other good things we would like in our lives but haven't reached us yet are what we usually need to consciously manifest for ourselves. I use these three gems to simplify the manifestation process for myself and if need be, I hope in some way it will do the same for you too.

- **Awareness.**
  - Awareness of that which we desire is for our greater good, that we deserve it, and that we can have it.
- **Faith or Belief.**
  - Faith or Belief that we deserve it and that there is a Universal or Supreme Force working with us to manifest our desire.
- **Intention with Conviction.**
  - Putting the intention out to the Universe with the complete conviction of Mind, Body and Soul that the manifestation is complete.

 "Through the window of my soul, I offer my intention.
Knowing that it will be done, strengthens my conviction."

The Expectation

It has been my experience that the expected miracle can manifest in very different ways. From the direct, to a subtler influence, to forcing a paradigm shift in our lives that leads us to the change that influences the end result. It would be so much nicer to just sit back and let the razzle dazzle happen but that's not necessarily how life works. We have to play our part in the manifestation of miracles.

The Power of Faith

Healers through the ages have invoked Awareness, Faith and Conviction to do good and to connect us to our higher-selves. As a person and as a Holistic Therapist I am constantly in awe of and inspired by Jesus' miracles where the emphasis on Faith or Belief predicated miraculous healing.

The Gospel of Matthew recorded a miracle in which Jesus miraculously healed two blind men who followed him, asking for mercy.

As described in *The Gospel of Matthew*:

> As Jesus went on from there, two blind men followed him, calling out, "Have mercy on us, Son of David!"
>
> When he had gone indoors, the blind men came to him, and he asked them, "Do you believe that I am able to do this?"
>
> "Yes, Lord," they replied.
>
> Then he touched their eyes and said, "According to your faith let it be done to you;" and their sight was restored. Jesus warned them sternly, "See that no one knows about this." But they went out and spread the news about him all over that region.
>
> ~MATTHEW 9:27-31, NIV TRANSLATION

Believe in your own greatness. Manifest your own Soul Miracle. But most importantly, believe in yourself.

This chapter is dedicated to the miracles that have gone down in the annals of history, to miracles un-recorded, scoffed at, and most importantly miracles yet to manifest.

Thank you to my mum Kavita S. Kishinchandani, for your unconditional love and support. To my husband Anthony, for your contribution of verse. To the wonderful people at Visionary Insight Press, thank you for bringing it all together.

-Vandana Mendonca

Angela N. Holton

ANGELA N. HOLTON is a Life Coach, Workshop Teacher, International Speaker, Blogger for www.lovesanctuary.com, Host of Love Notes Podcast, and Best Selling Co-Author of "Whispers of the Heart". Angela is founder of Love Sanctuary, an inspirational platform committed to sharing positive and motivational messages on love, growth, and healing. Angela's mission through Love Sanctuary is to teach and inspire radical Self-Love, the key to living healthier, happier, and more purposeful lives.

www.lovesanctuary.com

Believe! Expect! Receive!

History has reported miracles since the beginning of time. Many are supported and detailed in different religious instruments, including the Christian Bible, the Jewish Torah, the Muslim Qur'an, the Buddhist 'Lotus Sutra' and the Hindu Bhagavad Gita, or Vedas. In the Bible, we learn of Christ turning water into wine in the Book of John and he is described throughout the text as having miraculously healed the sick, the lame, the blind, the maimed, and leprous. In the Torah, the Old Testament, God is known for the miracle of creation and other miraculous ways in which he used his people to create supernatural events, such as Moses parting the Red Sea. The Bhagavad Gita describes miracles as a fact of our nature. Once we live in higher consciousness, the state of enlightenment, then we embody the spirit of Divine and access our own divine abilities. Our lives become a reflection of God.

But miracles did not cease after ancient history. Miracles are alive and happening even today. We hear stories of modern day miracles occurring all the time, such as people healing from incurable diseases or Mother Nature continuously showing off her beauty and amazement in each sunrise and sunset, in each child that is born, in the flowers and trees that bloom, or the gust of winds and waves in the infinite sky and ocean. We may also know of miracles manifesting through the story of best-selling author and speaker, Anita Moorjani, who experienced a near death experience while in a coma, ravaged with Stage IV cancer throughout her body. By all scientific considerations, Mrs. Moorjani's body was "dead". Yet, she miraculously awoke out of her coma and within a few weeks, cancer was no longer found inside her body. We have also heard countless stories of babies and children that have survived fatal and catastrophic car and plane accidents, when by all accounts survival was very unlikely. Or when Jessica Morales, also known as Baby Jessica, became famous in 1987 after she fell down a well, with an 8-inch diameter, and remained trapped for 58 hours while the entire Nation watched. She miraculously survived by an extraordinary rescue effort. Or lastly, the 2015 true story told in the documentary, "Twinsters", of

South Korean identical twin sisters, Anais Bordier and Samantha Futerman, who were adopted separately at birth in South Korea and then raised on two different continents. Anais grew up in Paris, France, while sister Samantha grew up in New Jersey. But in spite of living worlds apart, Facebook and social media brought these two beautiful sisters miraculously and synchronistically together. Only a power greater than human forces could bring together two people out of the nearly 8 billion people on the planet, living 3,669 miles apart.

"You'll be happy to know that the Universal Law that created miracles hasn't been repealed."

~ DR WAYNE DYER

But, what about the miracles that are not necessarily monumental occurrences to the rest of the world or newsworthy, yet powerful, healing, and life changing to everyday people? What about the small and perhaps simple and practical, everyday miracles that happen to each and every one of us? Are these not miracles? Whether big or small, profound or mundane, I believe miracles are performed every single day. Like the Baghavad Gita and A Course in Miracles, I support miracles as a fact and function of our nature. Miracles are our birthright. Our Creation itself is a miracle, thus we have the entire Universe inside of us, capable of creating miracles of all magnitudes.

"No miracle can ever be denied to those who know that they are one with God."

~ A COURSE IN MIRACLES

As humans, we are the physical manifestation and the vessel through which Spirit performs miracles. God cannot be God without us. Nor can we witness or experience miracles without God. We are created in his image and likeness, therefore, we have the power within us to co-create miracles each and every day. Whether we are acting as a vessel to Spirit's miraculous energy, as a doctor, teacher, mother, or friend, we are the tools God uses to carry out his work. Spirit is always available to create miracles in our everyday lives, but it relies on us to manifest them.

A miracle, whether big or small, is a sign that God uses to point to Himself. God wants all the recognition, the praise, the glory, and the understanding that the power behind certain events transcends any human or natural law, and is only explained by a supernatural or Universal Law. Spirit also uses signs to communicate with us, so if we are paying close enough attention to our omniscient and omnipresent Creator, we will hear and manifest miracles all the time.

My Life of Miracles

I witness miracles daily in my life. Some may call them simple and mundane miracles, but I still call them miracles. Events that occur in my life that are beyond my power and understanding happen all the time. From synchronistic meetings to phone calls with people that offer insight or guidance to my greater calling. When we imagine all of the circumstances that must come together to align two "strangers" or friends to meet, at the exact same place, at the exact same time, and offer to one another a message or a sign that brings healing, understanding, or guidance to the other, is nothing shy of a miracle. Or when I dream of someone I have not seen or spoken to in a long time and I wake up in the morning to an email or call from them. Or when Spirit laid on my heart a calling to live by the sea, but showed no immediate signs or possibilities of it happening. Yet within a year of my intense envisioning and focus, I receive an incredibly unexpected email with an opportunity for me to move to a paradise island. I did not ponder or hesitate in my decision. I leaped at the opportunity because I knew that it was a miracle from the Divine.

One of my greatest miracles appeared a couple of years ago on a morning that I awoke incredibly sad, confused, and angry with God. I was intensely angry, so, I asked God the questions of who am I and why am I here? I commanded God to give me the reasons for my life and my purpose. And not only did I ask with insistence, "I" instructed God to give me an immediate answer, "Today". Not tomorrow, not next week, but today! I cried out, "If you are real God, as I have deeply believed, then I need you to show me today just how real you are. Show me your presence so clearly that it is unmistakable and undeniable. My faith is teetering God, so I need your answers, NOW!"

Following came a sudden and powerful push from my spirit, instructing me to leave my home immediately and head to a nearby café with my journal. So, I quickly brushed my teeth, grabbed my coat, and my journal and walked briskly across the street. It is impossible to describe in simple words, but there was a feeling that someone was pushing me out of my front door. The sense of urgency was palpable. Within only minutes of sitting in the café and writing in my journal, tears silently rolling down my face, a "stranger" leans over to me and asks, "May I pray for you?" Instantly, I began to sob. I asked this "stranger", "How did you know?" But, I already knew the answer before asking, so, I accepted this man's loving gesture for prayer. After his prayer and without any announcement, fanfare, or an introduction of any kind, he silently walked out of the café.

Meanwhile, a gentleman wearing a yarmulke sat nearby, observed our encounter and placed his hands in a prayer and raised them up, as if signaling to the power and grace of Our Almighty Universe. Shortly after, I visited this other "stranger", my angel and messenger from God, in his art gallery, and what commenced for three hours was my telling of my personal life's story, including my pains, my sorrows, my frustrations, my dreams and my visions. What he imparted to me that day was the beginning of the greatest changes in my life. Upon pouring out divine wisdom and reading sections of my journal, this Orthodox Jewish man, who I met all of a few hours before, instructed me to create a daily writing practice. He commented that I was an inspiring writer and that I have a message to share with the world, a greater purpose brewing inside of me that I have been unable to awaken. He believed the root of my pain and frustration in my own life stemmed from my inability to tap into and "birth" the creative and powerful energy that already existed within me. He said, "it doesn't matter what you write…just write." He finished by saying, "I believe one day you will have a book published."

I thanked him profusely for showing up as my miracle and spirit guide during my moment confusion and despair. I knew my life was forever changed. He planted the initial seed inside of me to begin writing, even though my direction remained very unclear. However, it was after the devastating loss of my nearly 14-year old dog, just a few short months later that God called me into my purpose to use my own life and my grief and pain to inspire others. Hence my life as a writer began. In nearly two years, I launched a spiritual business, wrote countless blogs on my website, co-authored two published books, wrote for online spiritual sites, become an online contributing blogger to the Huffington Post, host of my own podcast, taught over a dozen seminars and workshops, and moved to Paradise.

Now, you may be thinking my meetings with both of these gentlemen were mere coincidence. But I liken them to miracles. They both appeared "timely" on my path to offer healing and guidance to my life's purpose, instructions that only a supernatural and Divine power could know. But even more important, they answered any doubts I had about my faith. Upon my desperate and draconian request, God revealed himself to me so powerfully that day that my faith in God and miracles grew even stronger. I describe that unusual day as an unforgettable moment of powerful healing and transformation in my life. My life has not been the same since as I am currently living out my life's purpose on a beautiful island as a teacher, healer, and writer.

Believe in Miracles

 "Miracles happen everyday, change your perception of what a miracle is and you'll see them all around you."

~ JON BON JOVI

When we learn to believe, expect, and receive miracles, then miracles happen all the time. But they begin with a belief. Once you see everything as a miracle then everything will become one. As we witness more miracles in our lives, our faith naturally grows, increasing our expectancy of miracles, which in turn creates even more miracles to manifest in our lives. I awake each day not only asking for miracles, but also expecting them.

 "Expectancy is the atmosphere for miracles."

~ EDWIN LOUIS COLE

How to Manifest Modern Miracles

To manifest more miracles in your life, start off first by believing in them. Any doubt, mistrust, or apprehension will interfere with our natural ability to create them. If we believe, then we'll receive! If we dismiss synchronicities, divine interventions, powerful transformations and healing, as "coincidence", then we miss the entire point of miracles. Life will become one big coincidence to us rather than a witness and knowing of the incredible power we possess.

Once you have the belief and inner knowing that miracles exist and are happening to and around you all the time, then it's time to start creating more of them in your life. Like everything else in our lives, change and self-improvement happen initially through our own self-awareness and knowledge. Bringing mindfulness and attention to our lives facilitates our bearing witness to miracles. Are we aware of ourselves at any given moment? Of who we are? Where we are going? What we desire? What we are afraid of? What are our weaknesses and limitations? Our strengths? The more we know and understand ourselves the greater our ability to recognize and understand God's miracles as they appear through guidance, subtle offerings, simple and mundane gifts, and powerful synchronicities. As we come to fully know ourselves, we can no longer dismiss miracles as chance encounters or "luck", we can recognize that gifts are constantly being offered to heal and improve us, and guide us to our next steps.

Love Thyself!

The only thing that God ask of us is to Love each other and ourselves. To know God, is to know and Love thyself. The more we align with the Spirit and vibration of Love, the energy that creates miracles, the more miracles can flow easily and effortlessly into our lives. Love and acceptance are the magical ingredients to heal, change, or attract anything miraculous into our lives. Be love, not perfection, but Love. Love yourself unconditionally by embracing your strengths, as well as your flaws and imperfections. Nurture your heart and inner-child with kindness and compassion. The kinder and more loving you are toward yourself, the more loving you can be toward others.

Blocking Miracles

Fear and UN-forgiveness are our two greatest impasses to creating miracles. We align with Spirit and miracles through Love, our true nature. Fear, which lies on the opposite spectrum of Love, exist only so that we may know and feel the experience of Love. Fear can wreak havoc and disappointment in our minds and in our lives if we allow it to control and manipulate us. Although some fear may always be with us, we may use it as a tool to grow and to heal, and to elevate us to new heights. Fear is never intended to circumvent our belief in magic and miracles. If we allow it, fear may act as an albatross, holding us back, keeping us stuck, and shattering our belief in Spirit. But we can remember that God never places a dream inside of us that we do not have the power within us to create.

> "Miracles start to happen when you give as much energy to your dreams as you do to your fears."
>
> ~ RICHARD WILKINS

Un-forgiveness is the other deadlier poison to miracles. According to A Course in Miracles, "Forgiveness is 'our' function as the light of the world. It is 'our' forgiveness that will bring the world of darkness to the light." Forgiveness is our purpose. It is the reason we are here. Although forgiveness is a lifelong task, we can practice it every day in order to clear and open our hearts to receive God's miracles. We have all heard somewhere before that, "Un-forgiveness blocks our blessings." This is because un-forgiveness often turns into anger and resentment, which festers and blocks the heart and prevents us from aligning with Love. An unforgiving heart is a hardened heart and Miracles manifest through Love, suppleness and openness of the heart.

So, if Un-forgiveness burdens your heart, consider practicing each day releasing anger little by little. Release the object of your resentment, including yourself. Write a letter of forgiveness to the person you need to forgive and safely burn or discard it. This practice is a gift to yourself, to invite greater miracles into your life, as forgiveness is an act of self-love. Not an easy feat, but our lives are worthy of our commitment to its practice. Forgiveness is a lifelong practice. Be patient, gentle, and kind with yourself.

Worry About Your Own Backyard

How can we manifest or witness miracles if we are too busy lurking in someone else's life? We may worry not on how God is blessing someone else, but rather focus on our own lives and the miracles that God has in store for us. What is meant for us will be for us and no one else. If we are too consumed comparing, competing, judging, and observing another's life we may miss important guidance and miracles that are designed specifically for us.

I Am Thankful, So Very Thankful

A simple, yet powerful gratitude practice will help align us with creating miracles in our lives. Gratitude is an act of Love and creates a positive mindset. As we go about our lives with a spirit of thanksgiving, we are more apt to look for inspiration and miracles. Start each day with a gratitude practice. Write down 5-10 things you are grateful for each morning or evening. If you do not have time to write them down, whisper them in prayer and meditation.

It's a Bird, It's a Plane...It's...

Believe in the infinite possibilities of life, the unknown, and the outrageous. Believing that our Creator can make anything happen is the beginning and the end to manifesting modern miracles. See everything, from the moment you arise each day, as a miracle. Take note of them as they are happening. Write them down. Give thanks for them. Ask Spirit for them each day. Then ask for guidance to your miracles and an open heart to receive them. I begin each morning in meditation asking Spirit to reveal itself to me, to show me miracles. But asking is not enough, we must go out and search and make them happen by living in the moment and listening to our wise inner-guide and teacher. The whispers that Spirit brings to our hearts are messages to guide us to miracles.

 "There are only two ways to live your life. One is as though nothing is a miracle. The other is as though everything is a miracle."

~ ALBERT EINSTEIN

Wishing you the belief, expectancy, and manifestation of Miracles in your life!

Dedicated to all the angels, spirit guides, and teachers who continuously guide me to miracles. God bless you all!

Mom & Daddy, the depth of my gratitude could never be put into words. Your love for me blows my mind away. You are my angels on Earth and I can only pray that I love as unconditionally as you love me. I love you with all of my heart and may God always bless you! To the incredible matriarch of our family, Nana, your strength is unparalleled. You are the strongest, human force I know. Grandma, I love you! Aunt Carol, thank you. You never waver in your love and support for your Baby Girl! To my beautiful and loving sisters, Brigette, Erica, and Gabrielle. Thank you for always looking out for me, and the blessing of having sisters as friends. Jack & Chris, it's always been the five of us. My brother, Antonio, I love and appreciate you with all my heart. Cousin Pat, I love and appreciate you! To my amazing circle of girlfriends, my love tribe. You know who you are! You wipe my tears, you hold me hand, and you laugh through it all with me. I couldn't ask for better SisStars! Thank you to Igal Fedida and Dr. Dee Watts-Jones. My late Granddaddy, I love you. Kobi, my angel, you are always my inspiration and guide through all of it.

~ Angela N. Holton

Barbara McKay

BARBARA MCKAY studies the Science of the Mind at the Centre of Spiritual Living in Edmonton, Alberta. She lives with her son in Sherwood Park and loves her life. Barbara continues to be amazed at the wonder of the beauty and adventure within our magical Universe.

My Ford F150 XTR Super Crew

We are manifesting within every moment whether we realize it or not. Before I begin my story, let's look at what exactly does *Manifesting Modern Miracles* mean?

Manifesting

1. *a display or show (a quality or feeling) by ones acts or appearance, demonstrate or*

2. *evidence of proof*

Modern

1. *of or relating to the present or recent times as opposed to the remote past*

2. *a person who advocates or practices a departure from traditional styles or values*

Miracles

1. *a surprising and welcomed event that is not explicable by natural or scientific laws and is therefore considered to be the work of a divine agency*

2. *a highly improbable or extraordinary event, development or accomplishment that brings very welcome consequences*

I suppose this is probably the closest explanation to as what happened when I manifested, "Winning My Truck Experience." It was July of 2012 and I had been studying the Laws of Attraction and reading every self-help book I could get my hands on that spoke about how we create our own lives. My experience began before I even knew it was beginning.

It was a day like any other date, beautiful and sunny and not much was on my list of exciting things to do. So, when I had the opportunity to go for lunch with a friend, I said, "Yes." When the waiter arrived, handed me a menu, told me of the daily specials and recommended the strawberry salad, I said, "Yes." This was all it took to begin my journey down a path of Manifesting a Modern Miracle. You see, in saying "yes" to the things I loved, I was presented an entry form into a drawing to win a barbeque. At this time, I was experimenting with being a vegetarian, so when I filled out the entry form, I wasn't attached to the outcome of winning. I just thought, *wouldn't it be nice* and then I forgot all about the entry. About three weeks later, I received a phone call from the restaurant informing me I had won the barbeque and I was one of a maximum of 55 people entered to win a 2012 F150 XTR Super Crew truck. I may not have been that interested when I put my name on the entry form for the barbeque; however, the thought of winning a truck had caught my full attention.

After receiving a few details, such as when and where the drawing was to happen, I hung up the phone and immediately began searching my mind for all the instructions given to me from all the books I had read on laws of attraction. I took a moment to gather myself, looked at my schedule and cleared the rest of the day's activities. I knew I needed to take immediate action, to show the Universe, my Creator, I was serious when I declared this was MY truck. This was my opportunity to show myself that we are, in fact, creating our lives; no matter how big or small the request, we have the power to manifest our desires.

So I went to the closest Ford dealer and asked if I could test drive a white Ford F150 XTR Super Crew. I was told they had no white trucks, but I was welcome to test drive one of their many other colors. I had googled the contest after my phone call with the restaurant manager and the truck I was taking home was white, so I made my way over to the next dealership and found a white truck. I took my truck out for a ride, paying very close attention to the details of the dashboard, getting comfortable and blending into the interior as if I had drove this truck each and every day of my life. I began to notice that within my own vehicle the arm rest was much lower than the arm rest in my new truck. I smelled the new truck fragrance in and just appreciated the whole experience of driving a new vehicle. Then when I was done, I thanked the dealer and took a picture to place on my phone as a screen saver so I could look at MY new truck every day and claim it as MY own. For the next two weeks I wrote on Facebook about how I was going to manifest MY new truck. Every time someone told me not to "get my hopes up", I thanked them for *their* opinion and held strong to the knowing that this was MY truck. Every time I saw an F150 XTR Super Crew on the road, I said to myself, "Look! There is MY truck." Every time I drove my own vehicle, I would envision the dashboard of the F150 and I would pretend to rest my arm on the much higher arm rest of the F150. In my mind, it was MY truck and so I used one of the practices I had read about and decided to write about the experience of winning MY truck. This is word for word what I wrote:

> ***Me winning my Ford F150 XTR Super Crew experience.***
>
> *I walk into BP, unsure of where to be, yet filled with excitement. As staff direct me where to go, I walk with confidence & power of knowing Creator has lead me here. As formalities are conducted, I look at my new truck with appreciation & joy filled bliss. I accept my key & as my turn arrives, I walk up to my shiny new truck with eager anticipation knowing my key will start my new truck. As the truck comes to life, I realize the clapping & cheering that is going on. I say thank you, thank you to the Creator for living this wonderful and joyous experience in, as and through me. I say thank you to breakfast television & BP for hosting such a wonderful contest & I say thank you to Ford for building me such a beautiful shiny new truck. I also say thank you to all my friends and family who prayed for me & supported my beliefs throughout this blessed experience. As paperwork & formalities are conducted I feel a deep sense of love from the creator, gratitude filling the inner reaches of my soul & pure happiness in the knowing this beautiful truck is the testament of all my hard work, faith and devotion towards creating a different life with the Creator working in as and through me... And so it is! I love my new truck.*

As I said in the beginning, we are always *Manifesting Modern Miracles* whether we know it or not and manifesting the winning of this truck was one of the most pivotal days in my life up to that moment. For you see, it was within this experience that I not only won a truck, but I also won my life back because yes, it unfolded exactly the way I had wrote it. However, my prize was far greater than just a truck, it was the unwavering belief I could manifest anything if I put my mind to it. You see, I could have let doubt in when others tried to ease the disappointment in case I failed, but I didn't. I could have answered the call and did nothing to support the vision I wanted to create, but I didn't. I could have, at any time, thought to myself, this is silly, this doesn't work, but I didn't. It was within my unwavering faith and determination that I was going to make this experience mine and that provided the fuel for my experience to Manifest.

Euripides wrote in 450 BC, "One right thought is worth a hundred right hands". This experiment in which I had committed to (with faith and conviction) was the proof I needed. This was a new day, a new experience, a new way of being. I read a ton of books on manifesting and the Law of Attraction and what I discovered was this: within each book there were clues, bits and pieces on how to manifest one's desires. It was in the peeling back of all the layers of belief that it couldn't be done that brought this experience into my life in order to prove to myself that it **could** be done and I **could** do it! This one experience that I will draw upon for the rest of my days is the day I learned, without a doubt, we create our lives; we draw forth every experience to remind ourselves of our magnificent power within.

I began by following these steps as I have come to know and believe in them:

Step 1 - Ask for what you want

Step 2 - See your vision every day and claim it as your own

Step 3 - Be ready to accept your vision

Step 4 - Know your vision is already here

Ever since I manifested this experience (exactly the way I wrote it down), my life has changed in so many glorious ways I once couldn't even begin to imagine; however, I can say this: Marianne Williamson expressed, "A Miracle is a shift in perception from fear to love" and I believe this to be the pivotal link within my ability to Manifest Miracles within my life every single day. *Manifesting Modern Miracles* can come in all shapes and forms; it really does depend on our perception as to what it is we believe to be a Miracle. If a Miracle for you is wealth then, be prepared to uncover all your hidden unconscious beliefs that may be blocking the unlimited wealth you deserve. If a miracle for you is perfect health, then become a clear concise conduit to accept your vision. Whatever it is that you consider to be a Miracle and wish to draw into your life, be prepared to focus 100% of your attention on receiving without needing, but yet knowing it is yours to have when you just believe in the power within yourself. And remember, sometimes all we need to do is adjust our perception slightly and whatever it is we want to manifest is ours for the having. For that is what I have discovered to be the greatest manifested miracle within my own miraculous wonder filled life. Every day I wake up excited to be alive knowing the Universe is responding to me, as me and through me and let me tell you this is the true Miracle of life!

Love,

Avesha

For Wonder Woman…She taught me how to dream again.

Barbara thanks God for all.

~ Barbara McKay

Catherine Madeira

CATHERINE MADEIRA is a freelance writer and artist. She has been receiving ethereal information for years and is now sharing it in the hope of helping others in their life journeys.

Catherine is from the Reno / Tahoe area with her two children—Jason, who has always demanded an intellectual approach to life, and daughter, Kendal who was born a very old soul. Catherine has been a supportive, open-minded mother who allowed her eccentricities to expand. Subsequently, she has been able to receive, evaluate, and compile the information to pass it along to others.

Umbriel03@gmail.com

Structures of Life

Destination

Upon each days passing
I surge ever further from the perceived normalcy
Hurtling past new vision
In a direction that will not return me to where I began
But my unknown destination
Sought with good intent
Will surely prove to be the place
Where I belong

~ CATHERINE MADEIRA

Over the years, I have mentioned in my previously published books, I have had a myriad of experiences in the metaphysical world and have been given or shown information that remained anchored and at the forefront in my mind until I started documenting what I had received, only then was I able to deposit the formulas into my memory banks and move on with my life. It is no exaggeration that the thoughts will not leave my head until they are written down.

I was going through my writings trying to figure out what to share in this Book, Manifesting Modern Miracles. My mother thinks some of my writings get extremely complex. They are complex but the ideas and theories behind my work are very relevant, I just have to figure out how to make them more understandable.

For instance, one idea we will discuss in the future examines the speed of light compared to the speed of Vision, in the literal sense.

In this segment we are focusing on three aspects of our presence and growth. I will describe my out of body experience that led to much of the mosaic of teachings I receive. We will inspect the Aura and its function. And we will look at the living soul from a different position.

We will examine what the components of the soul are made of. Not the mist or the Light that people may witness, those are witnessing the soul as a complete living entity, but the actual structure and what each sub atomic element looks like. How the soul receives and retains experience and stores memories, how the soul is held together, how it is infinite and is literally a doorway to other dimensions. Just like the physical body is cohesive and appears solid, such as tissue down to atoms and genetics, and the anatomy. The soul also has a formation; I was shown what that framework looks like. It's a perfect system and its very simple, vast but simple. It may appear at first to be complicated and that is because it hasn't been introduced yet. But once it's explained to you it will be logical and easy to understand.

Let me halt here and slow down before this chapter turns into an Einsteinian night mare.

The Out-Of-Body Experience

In my most recently published book, The Empowerment Manual, I touched on the out-of-body experiences and the three different categories they are in. I mentioned that I would return to that subject and expand. Following that I move on to the duties of the Aura and the fabric of the living soul.

When I had my out-of-body, the type I experienced was a spontaneous and complete separation of my soul from my body. The Aura played a very significant role here. One of the points I learned during the experience is the function of the Aura. The Aura is basically the containment field generated by the soul to keep the soul contained inside of its current physical form or body. When my out-of-body experience began it was due to a partial opening of my field which allowed my soul to temporarily escape its boundaries. When you pass from this place the Aura, of course, is going to completely collapse and the soul leaves permanently.

I was lying on my back in bed when I had my life changing experience. I was beginning to fall away to sleep when all of a sudden I was hovering above an enormous pyramid. I know that may sound cliché but it is true. I was floating and directly above a complete pyramid with featuring the traditional top with a point. There was a light being projected from the top of the pyramid, a brilliant light, a prism. The rainbow of luminescence was being projected into the sky. I have actually seen this before, someplace, maybe in someone's artwork… I cannot remember where or when but I am certain I had witnessed it before. As the light cast from the peak… it enveloped me. I was very close to it, maybe 50 feet. I felt heat in this place, I believe it was day time as I could see the entire architecture cascading down and away from me. I still don't know why I was taken to a Pyramid, but I was absolutely there, directly above it and it was astonishing.

Then abruptly I was back in the room. What came next happened so fast I couldn't even process what was unfolding. But as most of us have experienced in moments of trauma, time slows down.

I felt a hole pass above me, (I didn't even know a hole *could* pass above me) and out I went. It was like I was sucked out. I now believe that was my Aura partially collapsing. Now that I have felt an opening in my Aura I can actually feel my Aura. Having the hole open up was much like standing in front of a window and opening it to feel the sudden windy chill hit your face. The Aura is a containment field, but feels more like a warm blanket protecting me. We don't sense it because it's always been there just like the flesh on our bodies.

We are so limited in our knowledge of the whole picture. But when my out-of-body initiated itself, it was as though the process knew what it was doing and I was just along for the ride. *Envision rocks, sitting happily on a mountain, a series of events occur that causes a landslide. Once the landslide is under way the rocks don't know why they have started rolling they just know they are rolling.* At the time, I was the rock. Following this out of body, I wasn't the rock anymore. Now I am the observer of the landslide and am able to view from a different vantage and understand cause and effect and share what I see. I am not shown why people are granted these exposures, as we all travel our individual journeys at different paces.

Previously I mentioned what came next. It's not super complicated. As I was sucked out of my physical form I went numb, because I wasn't present in the body so no nervous system to sense impulses. When I went numb it frightened me, then I felt myself lift off of the bed that scared me even more. I hovered there for a moment.

Then I took off. Moved down my body and legs then past my feet. I was seeing in all directions, no eyes to direct or limit the vision. Flying around the room completely out of control. I was trying in vain to reach the floor with my feet not yet realizing there were no feet… the same thing with trying to gain balance with my nonexistent arms. I wasn't high in the room I was just above the bed and desk. The flight pattern was chaotic counter clockwise circles. Very much like a full balloon that you let go of and watch throttle around the room. I had become flying confusion. It was anything but fun.

After a couple of moments of the pin balling around the space, I saw my body laying over on the bed. Once that happened, the instant I saw myself or my body it all suddenly snapped, clarity of the situation. I was "outside of me" and I began telling myself to '*go back, go back*.' The power of the realization caused me to gain control and the motion stopped. I slowly hovered back over to where I was laying and lowered down into my body. As I mentioned in The Empowerment Manual, the re-insertion was painful, it was quick but it did hurt because my nerve endings all reactivated. Full body pins and needles.

The split second I recognized I had left my body I gained control of my movement and was able to *will* my direction back to myself. If had wanted to, which I didn't... as I was terrified, I could have *willed* myself anywhere at that point. Movement at the speed of thought.

As I explained in my published article titled Adjustable Foresight in The Empowerment Manual book, almost instantly following this experience I realized that I knew things. Information was coming to me at will, it was similarly uploading spontaneously, without my seeking it. Knowledge, data and visions just started emerging and have been ever since. I ask a question and in time, using thought, the answer finds me.

Knowledge Gifted To Me At Will

One day I was sitting at my dining room table and all of the sudden this entire code popped into my head. I instantly understood the whole premise. I wasted no time and I rushed to get it down on paper. This is an example of the answers that found me without my request. What follows is that unquarried answer.

It was the system on how the mechanics of the living soul works. This equation is both simple and vast. All our living souls are made of a cohesive group of trillions of incomprehensibly small living units. Much like matter. For example, the human body is made of atoms packed together, but even though the body looks solid... it is not. Just like the soul, it is made of its living units loosely packed together. People that claim to see a mist or a glow or an apparition are in fact seeing a soul or spirit.

Super Sub Atomic Complex Living Array - SSACLA

If you could separate a single living unit from the trillions it is condensed with... it would look similar to the atom. It's made of an energy that we humans haven't yet discovered. It is five living components performing 11 different, yet connected functions. I have named this living unit (Super Sub Atomic Complex Living Array) or SSACLA.

The simplest way to explain this is, it absorbs, deposits and stores experience. Its function as a singular unit is simply to bank experience, every condition of every action, involvement, or sensory data available, color, sound, aroma, size, motion, temperature, objects small to colossal, incoming emotion, vibration, contact, etc. Every available aspect of input is consumed. It devours everything it experiences.

When you compile trillions of these ravenous SSACLA together a living conscious soul is created. When they are in the form of the soul their primary function is still to experience and store what they learn but also to react to, and interact with said experiences. To seek out all things, to love, to know pain, joy, anguish, fear, forgiveness, battle, empathy, excitement, wonder, and every experience imaginable. The job of the soul is to LIVE.

Since all souls are at varying levels of advancement it is impossible to declare intention because each soul travels in its own direction at its own pace.

The really interesting parts of this is if you could reduce your size to the equivalent of an atom compared to the size of the moon. If you could zero in on a single SSALCA unit and see it, as I said before it's not unlike the look of an atom, but if you could go even closer and *enter* the storage sphere of the SSALCA, you would be able to see and experience entire sum that that single unit has experienced since its incarnation at the beginning of the start of everything. In essence, you would be entering a new dimension or universe stored by this unit. In theory, one could walk through its eternal travels.

So each SSALCA has seen and had individual and different experience from all the rest, all of which each has stored eternally and separately. Then in the combined state, when you coalesce trillions of these units together and create a soul there, compiled knowledge is vast to the point of infinity. The GOD KNOWLEDGE the GOD ENERGY.

As souls move through our universe and dimensions and time, SSALCA units, for whatever reason, will be drawn away from the collective they have been joined with. They can and may attach themselves to a different living soul or souls and in doing this they share the information of the soul they just departed from. I believe that soulmates are a result of the exchange of SSALCA units from one spirit to another. In these cases, because the units witnessed and lived the same experience but have now split off to a different soul, both souls now have the same memories stored and will be drawn to each other. This also answers the theory that souls or spirits move in groups from one incarnation, time, or location to another, because they actually were all part of each other and prefer to remain close.

I am convinced that the great artists, writers, scientists, and mystics of this world are drawing memories stored in their living souls that their SSALCA's have picked up along their journeys.

Any & All

Any and all things
Born of the imagination
Surely do exist someplace
In the vast expanse of the Universe

~ CATHERINE MADEIRA

The Power of The God Energy

Now let's expand on what we have discussed today and talk a little about applying this information to Manifesting Modern Miracles.

You are extraordinary, you are incredible. Within your soul and your spirit is not only your conscious recollections of this life. But you walk the road also with the memory of the entire universe and all of 'Times' experiences and adventures.

Available to you are the secrets to seeing into other dimensions as well.

In mention of the Aura. Try to start sensing the warm blanket of your living Aura. Try to see the Auras in the world around you. These energy fields are visible. All you have to do is look to the outside of the object or being. Trees and birds in flight are the easiest to see when you first start trying. Try to watch a bird while flying with the blue sky behind, avoid clouds as backdrop as they may complicate your vision, you will see its energy field. It looks like a perfect circle around the bird. Trees are best at a distance at first, again with the blue sky as the backdrop, you will see their Auras.

In mention of information. Ask questions of the Universe, ask how things work, ponder these questions, focus on what the answers may be. Walk your question from its point of origin through to it conclusion. Always exercise this aspect of your spirit. The answers are waiting for you to uncover them.

Yes, humans are still limited in their ability to understand and access the powers available to them. Remember knowledge is power. Look for it.

I want you to believe in your dreams, and visions, and believe in your imagination. Write down new ideas, document yourself because what you have to say matters. The power of The God Energy is in you, accept your uniqueness and Manifest some Miracles.

Complexity

Seek not through avenues of complexity
Instead follow the path of logic and least resistance
To the place where your answers dwell.

~ CATHERINE MADEIRA

Dedicated to my Granddaughter Harlo Monro (the sweetest little girl in my world) who reintroduced me to the gravity of life. To my two tiny dogs, Bell, my best friend and angel on Earth, and Bee, Bell's lively assistant. My father, Richard, who passed years ago, but has stayed to watch over me.

I am grateful to my mother, Lilas Hardin, for her many years of support and for helping me lay out this particular Chapter. I also want to thank Lisa Hardwick and Chelle Thompson of Visionary Insight Press for seeing who I am. I love the editing suggestions you made and I so appreciate you helping me get my message across accurately.

-Catherine Madeira

Connie Queen

CONNIE QUEEN is a writer, mentor, life coach, trusted confidant and ally—partnering with others who are committed to growing spiritually, mentally, and emotionally on this journey called life. A generous listener and sounding board when making important life decisions, she is an energetic motivator towards taking action in accomplishing desired outcomes. There are no problems, only situations and circumstances, for which there exist a limitless supply of universal possibilities.

She believes all the answers one will ever need to live the life they want to live will be found by tapping the Divine Wisdom within.

connie@conniequeen.com
www.conniequeen.com
https://www.facebook.com/CQueensCorner/

Journey To Love

Much of my life had been spent living in the complaint of what I perceived was missing or wrong, rather than being grateful for what I already had. I would change situations and circumstances to no avail, constantly ending up with the same results. Insanity. It was not until I found myself slap dab in the middle of a third divorce that I faced the stark realization I was the common denominator in all my dysfunctional relationships. Yikes! Now that is a bitter pill to swallow. All I really ever truly wanted in life was to be loved and needed. So, why now at this point in my life, did I once again find myself feeling unlovable, hopelessly alone and desperately lonely? All attempts to fill the hole in my soul by altering outside conditions had ended badly.

The survival tools that had brought me thus far were failing miserably. Navigating life with a set of made-up stories resembling the fairy tales of my childhood, about how I perceived life *should* be, I had arrived at a place of disillusionment and a greater loneliness than my soul had ever known. The pain of the pain had finally become greater than the pain of the change. I had received the gift of desperation.

I had to change. But, what was I to do? The journey to love and happiness is an inside job. The key I discovered that unlocks the pathway to Divine Manifestation on the broad highway of life, allowing magical, miraculous things to occur, is action and more action.

Open Your Heart to Self-Love

To be in love is a grand and glorious thing. Ending a love relationship can be an equally devastating experience. By the end of my third marriage, I began to think that there was something innately wrong with me. I thought I must be incapable of loving another person or worse yet, I was unlovable and would never, ever, ever be happy. Then, while participating in the Heal Your Life® Workshop Leader Certification course, I had a defining moment. Oh, my gosh! It wasn't *them* I didn't love. It was *me!*

How was I to find this love of self? Mirror work is a powerful technique for helping learn to love and approve of oneself, as well as for making wonderful steps forward in life. Mirror work creates a twelve-inch drop by getting out of my head and right into my heart and emotions. Often, tears will start to fall as you connect with yourself at a deep level. That's okay. Let them flow. It's cleansing and freeing.

Stand in front of the bathroom mirror and look into your eyes. Stay focused on your eyes. What feelings and thoughts do you have as you do this? Are you immediately critical of your physical appearance? Do you have positive feelings about yourself? Say to yourself, "I love you, *(your name)*. I really, really love you." In the beginning, if that is too difficult, say, "I am willing to love you!" It is challenging for most people to look in their own eyes and say, "I love you!"—first of all because for many individuals it is not yet true, and secondly, the majority of us were taught that loving yourself is vain and selfish, which is also untrue.

Keep reinforcing the use of mirror work. Celebrate progress made by asking yourself, "What can I do for you today? What can I do for you today that makes you happy?" Wait for the answer AND then do that special thing just for YOU today! Doing mirror work every day creates quantum leaps of transformation in your life!

Uncover Limiting Beliefs

A daily practice of mirror work uncovers more and more negative messages permitting us to take an even deeper look into ourselves and our core belief systems. We want to continue to reinforce our positive beliefs while identifying those negative ones that keep us feeling stuck. These nasty little devils are hidden right below the surface, sabotaging any real chance at happiness. This is not your fault. We are blind to them. It is impossible for us to change any limiting beliefs unless we know what they are.

In her book *Love Yourself, Heal Your Life® Workbook*, Louise L. Hay offers a series of exercises "*Who Are You? What Do You Believe?*" that were revolutionary on my road to living an abundant life full of limitless possibilities. Though simple, it is not always easy to look at the past. It is my perception of my life experiences and how I reacted to them that created ALL my seeming problems. Take responsibility. Name it, Claim it, Change it!

It does not always feel good at the time AND, yet, it is so worth it. Trust me… you have to dig to reach the gold!

 "I am willing to release all old negative concepts and beliefs that are no longer nourishing me."

 "I see myself with eyes of love and I am safe."

Experience the Freedom of Forgiveness

It would be so effortless to continue to blame everything and everyone for the emotional pain and suffering I have endured, if it were not for the fact that the incident is long over and I am the one who still suffers. An expression that rings true for me is "resentments are like taking poison and expecting the other guy to die."Anger turned inward creates self-pity and depression. It is such a slow death. The self-destruction anger creates in all our relationships and body is insidious. The good news is that by accepting responsibility that you are the source of all dis-ease, you are free.

However, in order to be truly free and open to love, this unresolved anger towards those closest to us requires purging at a deep level. One way of addressing these resentments is to compose a handwritten letter to dad, mom, brother, self, partner or former spouse. Squeeze out every feeling of hurt, disappointment, rage, and sadness, telling them precisely how angry you are, being sure to list the actions that were at the source of those feelings. Really vent, holding nothing back. When finished, sit down in front of a mirror. Be sure to have tissues nearby. Look into your own eyes and visualize the other person. Read them the letter voicing why you are so angry. When you are finished, tell them, "What I really want is your love and approval." "I am willing to release the need to be an angry human being." Notice if you have any hesitation in your willingness to let go of the past and whether or not you want to hang on. Fold the letter and write on the outside, "What I really want is your love and approval." Burn the letter.

By giving up the right to punish myself and others, I am free. I experience freedom from and freedom to. Freedom from fear of people, of commitment, of failure, and rejection. Freedom to be loved. What a joy!

I'm free . . . What's Next?

Make a List of Must Have's and Can't Stands

I had little experience with what it looked like to go out on a date. I was very familiar with getting married; but, lacked any knowledge of what it looked like to date. I took hostages!

In the past, I had an idea of what it was I was seeking in the next Mr. Right. Now based primarily on what had been missing in the most recent relationship, it was quite easy to bring into focus my complaints about "him" that just bugged the crap out of me. So, I would look for someone who was "NOT" that. And, what that got me was another one just like the other one. The insanity continued because "NOT" is an invisible word. The focus was still on the negative aspects of the previous relationship.

As I was bewailing the sad state of my current affairs, my dearest friend came up with a novel idea. She suggested I write a list of the "10 Must Have's and 10 Can't Stands" that I was looking for in the ideal mate. She said "good daters" always carry with them a mental shopping list of traits they "must have" in a mate, and traits they "can't stand." She reminded me that dating is about "gathering information," NOT finding someone to marry; so, seek wise counsel and pray about it.

Becoming crystal clear about these characteristics armed me with the information to know with confidence and clarity whether a potential partner was worth pursuing. If you think it's important to have a shopping list when you go to the grocery store, it's a thousand times more important to have a shopping list when you're looking for a partner.

So, what should go on your list? That all depends upon you. For instance, people who pray frequently, have a close personal relationship with God, attend church, and are convinced that the development of their spiritual life matters more than anything else that they need to put SPIRITUAL PASSION at the top of their must-have list in capital letters. If you keep your house, car, and desk clean and spotless—and if it's important that your spouse share your passion for neatness—put this on your list. If you hate smoke, you should put "smoking" or "all addictions" on your can't-stand list. If you are super ambitious, and if you get bored by complacent, apathetic people, write "must be a go-getter" on your list. If you have a need for fun and laughter, be sure to include "great sense of humor" on your list.

You've got to spend plenty of time pondering, contemplating, and soul-searching. After carefully sorting and sifting all your likes and dislikes, your preferences and aversions, write them all out. Make a long, detailed inventory—and then narrow it down through a process of elimination. Your goal is to end up with a total of twenty ***non-negotiable*** items.

She told me non-negotiable is exactly what it means! If you can't find a person who has all 10 Must Have's and none of the Can't Stands then RUN, the other way before lowering your standards. And here's the underlying belief, should you be tempted to give up on your dream: "I want to get married! I need to get married! Therefore, I have to settle for less. After all no one is perfect and a less-than-ideal man (or woman) is better than no man at all. I am not worthy and deserving of having all my dreams fulfilled." She lovingly encouraged me to discover the kind of individual I needed in order to be really, really happy.

After making my list, I reported back to her with great pride and confidence in a job well-done. I suggest finding a friend just like her whom you trust. She is a most generous listener. She created a safe space where I was free to be totally vulnerable. Because, after all, I was about to lay my heart on the table. Over our cups of hot latte and after inviting God in, I revealed my heartfelt desires. Pausing just the appropriate amount of time for the greatest impact, she reviews the list, places her hand upon it and slides it back across the table to me. I'll always remember her exact words—"Now become that person. When you become a whole woman no longer searching for a man to complete you, God will grace your life with a whole man to stand beside you. You will be two whole people coming together to create a third entity called a relationship with God at the center."

I was speechless! What a concept! I spent the next five years doing exactly that.

So, you can imagine that no one was more surprised than I when, in the winter of 2009, as my husband Ross and I were packing up our house in preparation to retire in Mexico that I came across my list. It was at the bottom of my God Box. My husband was everything on my list. And, so was I! We have a beautiful, loving, lasting marriage with God at the center. Remarkable things, better than we could have ever planned, come to us because we put ourselves in God's hands. We presently live in a new and wonderful world, no matter what our present circumstances, by walking day by day on a path of spiritual progress.

Make the list! Pray giving it to God! Put it in your God box and keep praying until the miracle happens! More importantly, pray for peace, and the willingness to be a whole person despite your current relationship status. My sincere prayer is that God gives you the grace to live your life to its fullest! It will manifest! Miracles do happen! It happened for me AND it will happen for you, too!

God has the PLAN! All that is required are a few simple actions and that you BELIEVE!

Dedicated to all those who have loved and lost. Even though you told yourself it is too risky to love again, it is now time to believe that the opposite is true. Open your heart to love. Your true security and safety comes from trusting and cherishing your own heart.

I would not be the woman I am today without my bestest girlfriend in the whole world, Marjorie Amigone, at my side. Through tremendous joy and gut-wrenching pain, we have laughed and cried our way to an unbelievably glorious life. I know whenever I call, you will always be there. You know the "real me" and love me anyway. For you, dear friend, and your unconditional love, I am forever grateful!

-Connie Queen

Lisa Spooner

LISA SPOONER is senior marketing manager at an international restaurant concept, serving as strategic and tactical resource to franchisees for implementation of local multimedia and grass-roots campaigns.

She resides near Dallas, enjoying a variety of activities—particularly, spending time with family locally and in Oklahoma City. Lisa is also a licensed Heal Your Life® Coach, Workshop Leader, and Heart-Centered Business Seminar Facilitator. Through her practice, Authenticate You, she empowers people to discover, be, and enjoy their best self.

lisa@authenticateyou.com
www.authenticateyou.com

 Tending Mind's Garden

How many times have you envisioned yourself someplace seemingly unattainable—and remembered the feeling of imagining being there, after arriving at that destination? How often have you thought about someone that you haven't seen for a while and, "out of the blue", that person calls—or you run into them at some random venue? When have you done something because you thought (and, ultimately, *believed*) that you *could* do it? Every familiar thing—from pulp pressed into surface for accepting ink to become pages in this book, to computers used for composing and reading its contents—was once a thought... every thought is a seed in mind's garden.

Bountiful Soil

God, the Universe, Spirit, Source—is the richest and most responsive growth medium; bounded only by limitations that we construct, or those built by influence of people and other external factors that are allowed. Being aware of continuous connection to this vast expanse is essential for cultivation of fertile ground; the phrase, "conscious consciousness" is my plow blade—used to till by being mindful of thoughts and words (particularly "I am... ", the definitive that directs what we manifest; consider replacing with "I feel... ", a temporary state which can change), making adjustments in order to communicate intentionally; changing thoughts when needed. Speaking lovingly, encouragingly, often—silently, as well as aloud—to the unique expression of the Divine reflected in the mirror, excavates stones of doubt which undermine confidence and inhibit growth. Forgiveness of self and others—acknowledging that (regardless of the infraction, real or perceived) we are each doing the best at any juncture of life's journey based on previous harvests of mind's garden—is necessary to excavate deep-seated boulders which obstruct the loam.

Quality Seeds

Select carefully, when considering what to sow in mind's garden; choosing thoughts with greatest opportunity to reap yields of the desired outcome ... just like physical equivalent, planting an acorn and expecting a rose bush will result in disappointment. Balance the variety with color-filled blooms of peace, joy, happiness, love; sustenance, in the form of knowledge; fruits of information—being aware that, while many are sweet and refreshing, some can cause growth of dark entangled vines that may be poisonous—eradicate, or seek support in doing so, if these thoughts have propensity to become harmful or dangerous to self or others. Mind's garden extends infinitely, possessing more than enough space for bushes lush with abundance and prosperity, budding into unexpected (and sometimes unrecognized) blessings; saplings as well as ancient trees, standing alone and in groves—pillars of belief and ideology some of which may require pruning, trimming, or being cut down to clear space for new growth.

Regardless of the seed, one act is required for its success in taking root, sprouting, and growing: Faith ... *knowing*, with absolute certainty, that the thought or desire *will* take root and grow (another reason why it is important to be aware of, and eliminate, dark vines), in its appointed time ... which may not be the span that we think appropriate. Acknowledge its place on the landscape with gratitude; don't dig it up by lingering and questioning growth's unseen progress.

Nurture

While standing under the shower, water flowing over your head ... eyes closed, attention in the moment; visit mind's garden, dismissing intrusion of distractions (like reviewing to-do list or appointment schedule), as two molecules of hydrogen combined with one molecule of oxygen join others in a refreshing cascade of cleansing and renewal. Hydrate thoughts with focus, in appropriate amounts—neither drought nor saturation, throughout the day.

As love, joy, optimism, and gratitude beam sunrays over mind's garden; its landscape is, by function of equilibrium, also visited by occasions of overcast—disrupted by turbulent winds of sadness, frustration, disappointment, grief, anger ... often having fear as companion. Dark is necessary for light to exist and prevail. How long we sit in a downpour—whether we respond to inclement circumstance by seeking shelter and helping speed up its passing, or by remaining in the eye of the storm—is our choice.

> Sometimes when you're in a dark place you think you've been buried, but actually you've been planted.
>
> ~ CHRISTIE CAINE

Regularly identifying weeds and clearing brambles that tend to thrive in cloudy conditions or overgrown parcels, threatening to choke new seeds as they take root and begin to sprout, is challenging but necessary maintenance; thorny encounters, painful momentarily, or for an extended period, can heal. Tears cleanse mind's garden from inside out, providing emotional release and purge of stifling toxins.

Feed often, with affirmative prayer—knowing that seeds of thought sprout, grow, and flourish more bountifully, with intention.

Pollination

Seedlings spread by floating on the gentle breeze of quiet moments; many combining to produce hybrids more robust than each would be, individually. Infinite varieties of hue flourish wildly, side-by-side with orderly placement of sections arranged by strategic planning.

> Life isn't about finding yourself. Life is about creating yourself.
>
> ~ GEORGE BERNARD SHAW

Attempts to germinate new and seemingly viable strains are, occasionally, unsuccessful; despite tender care, or because of it, some sprouts do not surface—others wither shortly after pushing through ... often, expressed by physical sensation of "gut feeling". We, all, experience connection with Source, referred to by various terms: coincidence, luck, happenstance, God-tap ... intuition. The arrival of seeds whose growth might disrupt mind's garden is often preceded by, or together with, a feeling of physical unease meant to convey lesson, message, or warning—important to be noted for future reference, or acted upon—more immediately.

Harvest and Share Abundance

Harvests of mind's garden are displayed as reflection of Spirit ... in, as, and through each of us. An added bonus to the development and growth that we experience—achieving personal goals, attaining professional pursuits, exploring and traveling spiritual paths—every interaction presents opportunities to share the abundance, beauty, and diversity of mind's garden by communicating, learning, teaching, serving, creating art, making music, exchanging ideas, listening, collaborating, cooperating, enlightening, searching for cures, seeking to better understand each other.

You have just read harvest of mind's garden... fruition of a young girl's love of written expression, connecting through words and experiences with the intention to inspire; seed planted and tended for more than four decades—growing skyward, fragrant blossoms opening one-by-one and reaching toward the sun.

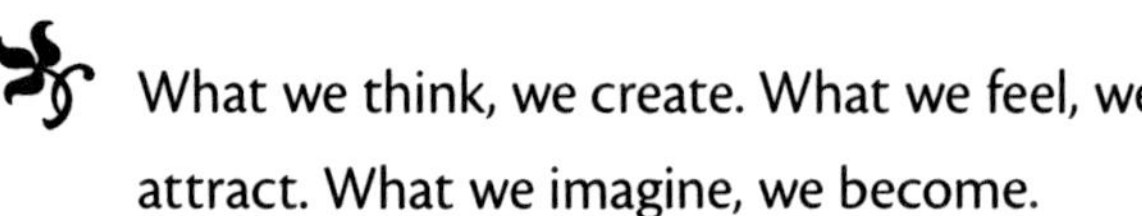

What we think, we create. What we feel, we attract. What we imagine, we become.

~ UNKNOWN

Dedicated to Mom, Linda, and Winter... words fail to express the depth of my gratitude for your love, encouragement, and support.

Thanks to "Core Council", as well as my village of family and friends, the importance of whose enthusiastic encouragement is beyond measure; to teachers, Dr. Patricia L. Crane and Rick Nichols, and Teacher-Teachers for guidance and embodying the Heal Your Life® philosophy, and for sharing Louise Hay's message around the world; to my HYL family for your contributions to helping people embrace and enhance the beauty within. For the strong and talented women who fostered my interest in artistic and written expression since childhood, I am eternally grateful.

~ Lisa Spooner

Bibliography

A Course In Miracles, Foundation for Inner Peace

Alfie. Gilbert L Dir. Paramount Pictures, 1966

Bhagavad Gita (English Translation).

Black C. *Alfie*. Bacharach B & David H. Parlophone, 1966

Crane, Patricia J. *Heal Your Life® Coaching Manual*. Bonsall, California: Heart Inspired Presentations, LLC. 2011.

Futerman, Samantha & Miyamoto, Ryan (Directors). (2015) *Twinsters* [Documentary Film]

Hay, Louise, L., *Love Yourself, Heal Your Life®, Carlsbad, California: Hay House, Inc. 1990.*

Hay, Louise (1984). *You Can Heal Your Life*. Carlsbad, CA: Hay House, Inc.

Hay, Louise L. (1991). *The Power is Within You*. Carlsbad, CA: Hay House, Inc.

Hay, Louise L. (2004). *I Can Do It*. Carlsbad, CA: Hay House, Inc.

Hay, Louise L. *Heal Your Life Training*, http://www.healyourlifetraining.com/teacher-training/

Hopkins, Emma Curtis. (1974). *Scientific Christian Mental Practice*, DeVorss & Company. Camarillo, CA

Makus, Marian, Editor, (1993). Collins Gem Dictionary and Thesaurus, Great Britain, Harper Collins p. 357

Melmed, Laura Krauss. (1998). *I Love You as Much …* (H. Sorenson, Illus.). Harper Collins Publishers. Inc.

Moorjani, Anita. (2012). *Dying To Be Me: My Journey from Cancer, to Near Death, to True Healing.* Carlsbad, CA. Hay House Inc.

Morris, Carla. "What Are Your "10 Must Have's and 10 Can't Stands" When Thinking About Dating/Mating for Marriage." *The Carla Morris Show.* 16 March 2012. http://carlamorrisshow.com/carlas-blog/what-are-your-20-must-haves-and-10-cant-stands-in-an-ideal-mate-for-life.

Quinlan, Mary Lou. "Inside the God Box." *Real Simple Home & Lifestyle Network.* 2016 http://www.realsimple.com/work-life/family/relationships/inside-god-box.

Tolle, Eckhart. (1997). *The Power of Now: A Guide to Spiritual Enlightenment.* Vancouver, B.C.: Namaste Publishing Inc.

Williamson, Marianne. (1993), *A Return to Love: Reflections on the Principles of A Course In Miracles.* New York, NY . Harper Collins.

A Call For Authors

Most people have a story that needs to be shared. Could you be one of the contributing authors to be featured in an upcoming compilation book? As a result of becoming a Published Author, some of the Visionary Insight Press contributors are now writing and speaking around the world.

Visionary Insight Press is leading the industry in compilation book publishing and represent some of today's most inspirational teachers, healers and spiritual leaders.

Their commitment is to assist this planet we call "home" to be a place of kindness, peace and love. One of the ways they fulfill this promise is by assisting others with the sharing of their inspiring stories and words of wisdom.

They look forward to hearing from you.

Please visit

www.visionaryinsightpress.com

Visionary Insight
PRESS

CPSIA information can be obtained
at www.ICGtesting.com
Printed in the USA
LVOW12s0421250316
480613LV00001B/87/P